AFTER THE
PICTURES

*Liverpool area cinemas.......
And what became of them*

Keith G. Rose

ISBN 13: 978-0-9554737-2-2

Printed and Published by Alba Printers Ltd.
1 St. Michael Street, Dumfries DG1 2QD

AFTER   THE   PICTURES

The Astoria, Walton Road, at night and in March 2009.

The former Derby Cinema on Scotland Road as a 1960's showroom

INTRODUCTION

The concept for this book began with the demolition of the Bedford Cinema in Walton, which I used to frequent as a child. "Going to the pictures" was an important part of our social history, a brief escape into another world, but the buildings that the films were shown in deserve to be remembered as well.

Photographs of a lot of the cinemas did not officially exist, but after a lot of 'thinking outside the box', pictures of almost all of them have been found. Surviving former cinema buildings have also been photographed inside and outside, some for the first and last time. The first part of the book is the history of the cinema in Liverpool and case studies of typical examples. A gallery of the cinemas is the second part, with brief details on them and plenty of pictures. This is not a boring history book, full of dry facts, but a celebration of a vanished part of Liverpool life. Please enjoy it.

Keith G. Rose, Scotland, 2011

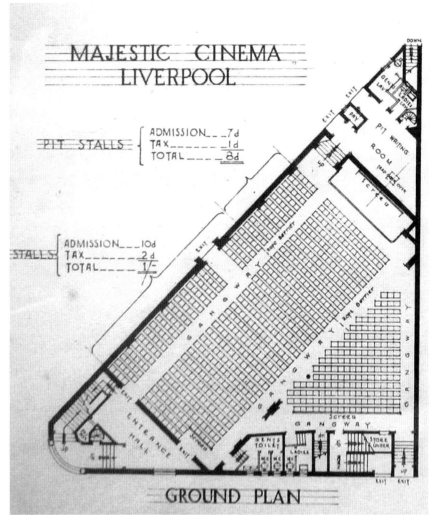

MAJESTIC CINEMA LIVERPOOL

PIT STALLS
ADMISSION ___ 7d
TAX _____ 1d
TOTAL ____ 8d

STALLS
ADMISSION ___ 10d
TAX _____ 2d
TOTAL _____ 1/-

GROUND PLAN

THE CREDITS PAGE

There is no chance that a work like this could be compiled without help, so I wish to thank;
The long suffering staff at the Liverpool Records Office,
Ted Bottle,
Cheshire County Cinemas,
Tom Heath ,
"Dusashenka",
Philip G. Meyer,
J & A Entertainments,
Merseyside Fire And Rescue Service,
Derek Minsull,
David Parr,
Mike Taylor,
Roger Shone,
The Walton History Group,
Dave Rogers
The North West Film Archive
Anyone else that has helped in any way.
Last, but not least, my poor wife, who has had to suffer years of cinema mania!

These plans show the layout of the Majestic in Daulby Street.
Note the offset auditorium to the screen, due to site constraints.
The layout of the projection suite and the staff rooms behind the stage are of interest. The layout gave the maximum picture size and throw.

SEATING PLANS

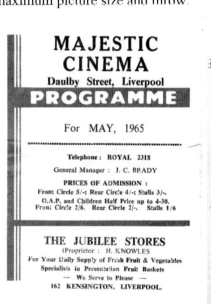

MAJESTIC CINEMA
Daulby Street, Liverpool
PROGRAMME

For MAY, 1965

Telephone : ROYAL 2318
General Manager : J. C. BRADY
PRICES OF ADMISSION :
Front Circle 5/-: Rear Circle 4/-: Stalls 3/-.
O.A.P. and Children Half Price up to 4-30.
Front Circle 2/6. Rear Circle 2/-.   Stalls 1/6

THE JUBILEE STORES
(Proprietor : H. KNOWLES)
For Your Daily Supply of Fresh Fruit & Vegetables
Specialists in Presentation Fruit Baskets
— We Serve to Please —
162 KENSINGTON, LIVERPOOL.

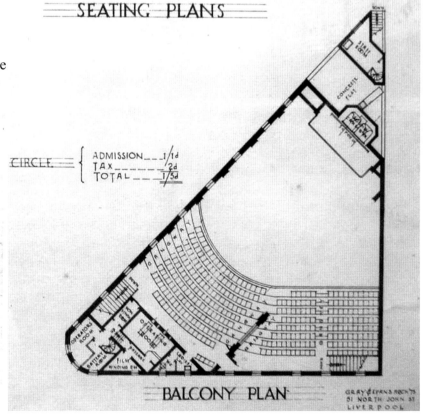

CIRCLE
ADMISSION ___ 1/1d
TAX _____ 2d
TOTAL ____ 1/3d

BALCONY PLAN

GRAY & EVANS ARCH'TS
51 NORTH JOHN ST
LIVERPOOL

MOVING PICTURES - THE GREAT ILLUSION!

This must be the biggest con in the world! Because our brain retains an image for a short period after the eye has ceased to see it(known as persistence of vision), if a sucession of still images, each slightly different, are viewed at a fast enough speed then the brain interprets them as movement. Good examples of this effect are the "flicker" books, where rapidly flicking the pages would make simple characters move, also the hand operated "What the Butler Saw" penny arcade machines,which came later and used a sucession of still photographs.

With the rapid development of photography, in the latter half of the 19 th century, it was only a matter of time before projectable "moving pictures" were invented. Early attempts were hampered by the lack of a suitable flexible base that would accept a photographic print, until the invention of cellulose nitrate and preventing flickering of the picture, as the film frames were intermittently pulled through the camera/projector.   Projecting a large image was limited by the lack of a powerful light source, until the electric arc lamp was developed in a compact form. By the end of the century, all the problems had been overcome and the cinematograph projector had appeared, the basic format of which is unchanged to this day. Television later used the same principle, but using a moving beam of electrons to scan an image on to the inside face of a cathode ray tube, which was coated to make it visible. The transmission rate was 25 images per second.

A brief description of how a film is projected, would help the reader to understand how their brain is fooled!

Sound film is projected at a speed of 24 frames per second. That means that the time taken for the frame to stop in line with the light source and the next one to be pulled into position is 1/24 of a second. Each frame of the film is therefore stopped in line with the light source for 3/96 of a second and the next frame is then pulled into position, but to prevent a flash of white light between the two, a shutter moves to block the light during the movement. This lasts 1/96 of a second(total time 4/96 or 1/24 sec.) When the next frame is projected, the shutter moves again, splitting the frame into two separate and same images. The interruption is also 1/96 of a second. This gives an actual image rate of 48 per second as the frame is viewed twice, which is above the rate of which the eye can see the separate pictures. It almost eliminates another vision defect, namely the ability to detect flicker. At 48 light interruptions per second , this is above our flicker perception. Silent pictures, projected at 16 frames per second, were subject to flickering, as anyone who has watched one, can verify.

The above method of projection is probably the simplest way to explain how it works, there are other variations, but the result is the same.

It is worth noting that films on DVD run at 25 frames per second. This is to make them compatable with the scanning rate of televisions. The downside is that the running time is 4% shorter than in the cinema, though some equipment now has a "cinema" mode, to play as the director intended.

BEGINNINGS

The first device that could really be said to have started projected moving pictures was Thomas Edisons "Kinetoscope" of 1889. It consisted of a peephole cabinet, inside which about 50 feet of illuminated film revolved on spools, the image being projected on to the end of the cabinet. Lasting less than a minute, the subjects were chosen to show movement, eg; a boxing match. Rather jerky, but a step in the right direction.

The first public showing of projected moving pictures took place on 20 May 1895, on the roof of Madison Square Garden, New York. Also that year, the Lumiere brothers of Lyon, France, exhibited their first projection machine at the first public film show in Paris. The first show in Britain, was on 20 February 1896 at the Marlborough Hall, London.

Next it was the turn of the showmen. Animated picture shows called "bioscopes" became part of fairgrounds. A highly decorated facade hid a simple tent. You paid your two pence and took your seat on a wooden form in the tent. Simple, short films were projected onto a screen, then it was over after a few minutes. Again, the film content emphasised movement. Quality was not what we now expect, but audiences loved it, making it a most profitable attraction! Early projectors were, like the cameras, hand cranked, but a good operator would soon develop a rhythmic action giving a steady speed. The light source could be limelight or a tungsten bulb if electricity was available. With this limited amount of light, the projector could not be placed too far away from the screen, thus limiting the picture size and brightness.

Just to explain, limelight was the popular name given to light produced by an acetylene lamp. These have a metal body with two vertical compartments, the lower containing calcium carbide and the upper water. A simple valve allows the water to drip onto the lime, producing acetylene gas, which burns with an intense white flame from a nozzle. They found favour for lighting theatre stages, especially the footlights and gave rise to the expression 'into the limelight'. Today, they are still used by cavers as a back up for their electric torches. The fire risk in the theatre was bad enough, but having one next to highly inflammable film was just asking for trouble!

In parallel with the showmen, films began to be shown in public halls and variety theatres. The public rapidly embraced this new form of entertainment, despite some church opposition, and the first decade of the Twentieth Century saw the new media achieve respectability.

DEVELOPMENTS ON MERSEYSIDE

The first films to be shown on the Wirral, were in 1896 at the Argyle Theatre, Birkenhead. Billed as the "Photo-Electric Sensation of the Age", they drew huge crowds and very favourable write-ups in the local press. For the shows, the theatre was wired for electric lighting, which was another attraction in its own right! To provide the electricity for the lights and projectors, temporary cables had to be laid through the streets, as the theatre only had a gas supply.

On the Liverpool side of the Mersey, animated pictures were shown at the Hope Hall, Hope Street and the Tivoli Palace, Lime Street, in May, 1896. James Kiernan, the Tivoli's owner, saw the opportunity to add this novelty item to his variety performances. The following year, bioscope pictures were a twice daily attraction at the Reynold Waxworks, below the Tivoli.

Early in the Twentieth Century, a travelling showman called A.D.Thomas arranged film shows in the Picton Hall, William Brown Street. To present them, he employed a local man, John F. Wood. This individual took over the shows at the Picton Hall and later rented the Queens Hall, Birkenhead plus Walton Baths for film shows. On the success of these, he decided to build Liverpool's first, purpose built, cinema, the Bedford Hall, in Bedford Road, Walton.

Another pioneer was Sydney Carter, who formed the New Century Animated Picture Company with a Mr. A. D. Sutherland. They exhibited at the Picton Hall as well, before opening the first permanent cinema, the New Century Picture Hall, in a converted Wesleyan chapel in Mount Pleasant. Mention should also be made of Leo and Fred Weisker who gave successful film shows at the St. Helens Co-op Hall. They went on to lease several Liverpool music halls, for conversion to cinemas.

Film shows had also been presented at other venues in the district, but these were of limited duration.

George Prince pioneered moving pictures in Bootle and beyond, presenting shows at the Sun Hall, Stanley Road, Bootle, in 1906 and the Waterloo Town Hall, in 1907.

THE FILMS

The earliest films were simple, short and made to exploit movement. A dog with a bone or a baby getting washed and dressed. Queen Victoria's funeral was filmed and proved that the public had an appitite for news. A bigger draw for the showmen was local scenes, the beach at New Brighton, busy streets, factory workers leaving, etc. The Lumiere Brothers sent their cameraman to Liverpool, where he captured "Liverpool Scenes of 1897", including the now famous dock views where the 'Cinamatographe' was filming from the front of an Overhead Railway train. When advertised, patrons would pack the hall in the hope of seeing themselves, or someone that they knew.

Everything had to be wholesome, as this was the establishing period for acceptance and respectability.

The recently restored works of Mitchell and Kenyon of Blackburn are a perfect example of the type of films produced. Even then, you couldn't believe all that you saw, because the firm faked Boer War scenes using Darwen Moor, even scratching the negative to replicate gunfire!

After 1903, the films became about 400 feet in length(5 minutes running time) giving more scope for drama. Whilst in the beginning, the exhibitors bought the film, we now see the practice of renting taking over. This made perfect sense for permenant locations, where once everybody had seen it, there was no point in owning it. For the travelling fairs, this did not matter as it may be the same film, but the location was always different.

There were hundreds of different film makers, as it was not that expensive to make films, especially if the public were your unpaid actors!

Programmes would be changed twice a week, plus a Sunday show once this was gradually permitted under the Sunday Entertainments Act of 1932.

SUN HALL, KENSINGTON, The Largest Hall in this Kingdom. Seating Capacity close on 6,000 Persons.

Commencing SATURDAY, JUNE 10th, at 8. Matinees Whit-Monday and Saturday, June 17th, at 3.

No Performance on Wednesdays,

THE STAFFORD GRAFTON ANIMATED PICTURE COMPANY,

Under the Most Distinguished Patronage and Presence of the

RIGHT HON, THE LORD MAYOR OF LIVERPOOL (JOHN LEA, Esq.) THE LADY MAYORESS, and Members of the City Council.

THE CHANNEL FLEET (under the Command of Admiral Lord Charles Beresford). *H.M.S. KING EDWARD VII.*

FRIDAY, JUNE 16th, AT THREE SHARP, SPECIAL MATINEE in Aid of the LORD MAYOR'S UNEMPLOYED FUND.

When the Entire Receipts will be handed over to the Fund. Special Programme—see other Bills.

FRIDAY EVENING *GRAND SPECIAL MILITARY NIGHT.*

Engagement of the Band of the 1st L.R.G.A. (V.), by kind permission of Col. T. G. Ewan and Officers, Conductor - - - Bandmaster C. T. Smith, R.A.

THE CELEBRATED EXCELSIOR VOCAL QUARTETTE,

Messrs. Forshaw and Evans, of the Liverpool Cathedral, in their Great Successes, Duets and Songs.

Popular Prices of Admission :—Gallery 3d. ; Body of Hall, 6d. ; Side Circle (reserved), 1s. ; Centre Circle (reserved), 2s. Note—No Early Doors. Seats may be now reserved at 1s. and 2s. at Messrs. Smith's Music Warehouse, Lord Street. Children Half-price to all parts (Gallery excepted). Doors Open at 7, Performance at 8 sharp. Matinees, Doors Open at 2, Performance at 3.

The Sun Hall on Kensington is a typical example of the public halls used in the early days. A screen would be erected on the stage, with the projector amongst the audience. Demolition photo's from 1956.

Theatres showed the films as a 'turn' and to clear the house! This is the Tivoli in Lime Street, later the Palais de Luxe. The gallery held the orchestra.

Queens Drive Baths was boarded over for dances and films. The projection room and port are seen in this demolition photo.

J. F. Wood was employed to run shows at the Picton Hall. He built the first purpose built cinema, the Bedford, in 1908 and built up a circuit.

THE CINEMATOGRAPH ACT OF 1909

Once it was realised that this was no passing fad, legislation was brought in, primarily to safeguard the public.

Up to now, the exhibitors merely set up their projector amidst the audience and showed the films onto a screen that could be as basic as a large sheet! The filmstock that was used at this time was cellulose nitrate, which was highly inflammable. If it jammed in the gate of the projector, or was otherwise exposed to high temperatures, there was a good chance that it would burst into flame, especially if the light source was a flame. With an increasing number of such incidents, the government had to act in the public interest. One of the main points of the act, was that the projection apparatus and films were to be physically isolated from the auditorium by being in a fire resisting enclosure or 'box'. There was also fire-fighting equipment and exits to be provided. (Stricter control proved to be needed and the Celluloid and Cinematograph Film Act was brought in. This did not apply in Liverpool because it was covered in the Liverpool Corporation Act of 1921.)

The importance of this act was that it put an end to the makeshift venues, whilst starting the building of purpose built cinemas. The stage was well and truly set for rapid expansion.

ENTERTAINMENT TAX

This was introduced as a temporary war tax in 1916. Like so many other "short term" measures, it remained in force until abolished on 10 April 1960. As it was levied on admissions and not profits, the net effect was to reduce the gross takings. Despite industry pleas, especially post Second World War when the decline in cinemagoing set in, it was not abolished before significant harm had been done to an already struggling industry. A lot of cinemas became marginally unprofitable, but without the tax they could have survived longer.

THE RISE OF THE PICTURE PALACES

The Cinematograph Act of 1909 became law on the 1 January 1910, Some of the existing buildings, like the former music halls, were altered to comply, but as the public had become enthralled by moving pictures, local businessmen saw an opportunity to not only build new cinemas, but make the buildings part of the whole experience.

The facades ranged from the functional to works of art in their own right. With often elaborate designs in stone or terra-cotta, canopies to protect queueing patrons from the elements and all brilliantly illuminated by the marvel of electricity, they really stood out against the mostly gas-lit streets. Once inside, a brightly lit foyer and pay box led to doors or stairs to the auditorium. In some cases, waiting rooms were provided, to keep the next performance customers warm and dry. Uniformed staff were on hand to assist all the way to your seat. These, except for the front stalls, were upholstered and finished in plush. Some halls had double ones at the rear, the purpose of which, the author had to grow up to find out! The auditorium itself could be richly decorated with a profusion of fibrous plaster mouldings in restful colours, leading the eye towards the front. Surrounding the screen was the proscenium arch. This, too, could be very elaborate and contained the curtains that covered the screen.

In front of the stage would be an orchestra pit, for the music to accompany the films. How many musicians there were depended on how up market the establishment was! Some owners hedged their bets, providing a stage big enough for theatrical productions and dressing rooms as well.

A cafe was provided in some of the larger establishments, but always, refreshments would be served to your seat during the interval.

All the main illumination was by electricity, but as it was a requirement to have uninterruptable secondary(or pilot) lighting in all public areas, gas was often used, especially in the smaller halls. The fireproof projection room was high up at the rear of the hall, totally isolated from it, with plate glass projection ports protected by steel shutters, that could be dropped in the event of fire. The whole building would be centrally heated by radiators from a coke fired boiler and ventilation would be by electric fans exhausting through ceiling grilles. The whole experience was of escaping into another world, before going back to your two up, two down terraced house, with its coal fire, gas lighting and an outside toilet!

Even the names of the cinemas were meant to inspire; Regal, Regent, Royal, Ritz, or a classical theme, Hippodrome, Palladium, Lyceum, Coliseum.

It is little wonder that by 1918, 63 cinemas had opened in the Liverpool area, increasing to 91 in the 1920's.

GROWTH OF THE CIRCUITS

In the beginning, it was individuals that organised the film shows. Once permanent venues had been established, some of the owners began empire building. The previously mentioned Weisker Brothers had already leased several music halls, for conversion to cinemas and with further aquisitions by 1914 had established a circuit, Weiskers Picture Palaces Ltd. They also operated as film renters. John F. Wood went on to found the Bedford Cinemas circuit by buying up existing halls. As more cinemas were built, other small circuits were created. But the major changes were to come from outside Merseyside.

A French film pioneer called Leon Gaumont started making projectors in 1896 and films the following year. These were marketed in Britain via an agent, who set up The British Gaumont Company in 1906. They started hiring films in 1907 and by 1922, it was wholly British owned and called Gaumont British! It was decided to start buying up existing circuits and building new cinemas. J. F Wood's Bedford Cinemas and Halliwell Hughes were two of the local companies aquired in 1928. This was not the end for Mr. Woods, who promptly formed Bedford Cinemas(1928) Ltd, which went on to build the Mayfair and the Abbey. Having gained a presence in Liverpool, Gaumont British started building new "super" cinemas. The first ones were called "Gaumont Palace", but later ones were simply "Gaumont". The new cinema in Oakfield Road, Anfield, was a "Palace" in 1931, but by 1937, the new one in Park Road, Dingle, was a "Gaumont".

Oscar Deutch started a chain of "Odeons" (derived from Oscar Deutch Entertains Our Nation, although the the word is from the Greek "Odeion", an ampitheatre near the Athens Acropolis), but only aquired the Paramount in

London Road in 1942, re-naming it Odeon. Both these circuits came under the control of J. Arthur Rank in 1941, but the government would not allow them to be merged until 1948, forming the Circuits Management Association. Thereafter a lot of Gaumonts were re-named Odeons.

Associated British Cinemas was set up as a subsidary of British International Pictures in 1928. The parent company made pictures and needed a readily available outlet for them. They, too, started aquiring existing chains and building their own. In Liverpool, Regent Enterprises, Savoy Cinemas (with a London head office), and several of the independently owned "supers" were taken over.

The final player arrived on the scene a lot later, but is included here for completeness. Soloman Sheckman was a former boxing promoter, from Newcastle. During and after the Second world war, he began buying up (usually cheap) cinemas. The company he formed to run them was called "Essoldo", derived from Esmond, his wife, Soloman, himself and Dorothy, their daughter. Two circuits with Merseyside cinemas, W. Gordon and Southan Morris, sold out to him in 1954, with one or two independents a year later. A total of some 240 cinemas, across the country, ended up under Essoldo control.

The advantages of a circuit was they had far more 'clout' with the renters. If also producing films, they had a guaranteed exhibition. There were also the economies that size produces. The downside of circuit aquisitions was that you ended up with the second rate halls, or "flea pits" as well. Essoldo ended up with a lot of this type due to buying at the bottom end of the market. It is reported that when Sol Sheckman was viewing the Liverpool aquisitions, he saw the Mere Lane and exclaimed "My God, what have I bought!"

THE "TALKIES" ARRIVE.

Until the end of the 1920's, all the films shown had been silent, with subtitiles. There was musical accompaniment of varying degrees, according to the standard of hall. Attempts had been made to include sound, such as Edison's "Kinetophone" system, trialled at the Grand, Smithdown Road, in 1915. This comprised the soundtrack on a record, which was syncronised with the projector. The record was played from the centre outwards and had an arrow marked 'start' for positioning the needle(if the needle stuck or jumped, the results could be quite amusing!). Finally, an optical soundtrack down the side of the film, was introduced from 1929 onwards. The film passed between a light source and a photo-electric cell, immediately after passing through the projector 'gate'. The variations in voltage, caused by the fluctuations in light passing through the sound track, were converted to sound frequencies, amplified and broadcast by a loudspeaker behind the screen. To achieve the wide range of sound frequencies, the speed of the film had to be increased from 16 to 24 frames per second.

Placement of the speaker sometimes meant moving the whole screen assembly forward, or building a sound chamber outside of the wall behind the screen. Another problem was acoustics. Some of the earlier halls were totally unsuited, resulting in terrible sound(like the Gem in Vescock Street!).

The first cinema in Liverpool to show sound pictures was the Olympia, at the start of West Derby Road. This had come under ABC control, with their takeover of Savoy Cinemas. The largest cinema in Liverpool, it was formerly a theatre and had a seating capacity of 3400. When Al Jolson in "The Singing Fool" started its run on 22 February 1929, even this capacity was not enough! Despite four performances a day, queues still stretched out of sight of the cinema!

Following this runaway success, rapid conversion to sound followed. One or two cinemas stayed silent as long as possible. The Palais de Luxe in Lime Street lasting until August, 1930. One of their advertising slogans was "Our pictures are still silent but sound". This, of course, meant the end of the orchestra's. In a lot of cases, the orchestra pit was incorporated into the front stalls, which is where the term, "pit stalls" is derived from.

THE SUPER CINEMAS

The 1930's saw the building of the so called super cinemas. These were to be the last word in luxury for their patrons. Most of them serviced the rapidly growing suburbs, even catering for another increasingly popular invention with a free car park for customers. Liverpool architects such as A. E. Shennan and Gray and Evans, already established in the cinema world, produced designs for most of them, at what must have been the pinnacle of their careers. The buildings were large(1000+ seats), with striking external features. What was not obvious, was that they were steel framed. this meant a lack of supporting pillars, or other obstructions to sight lines within the auditorium. Inside, the accent was on richness, in every detail. They were all built for sound, having no orchestra pit, but usually a theatre organ. Some were static, but others rose up in front of the stage, complete with playing organist(no, not like Monty Python!). Many had stages large enough for theatrical use and incorporated dressing rooms, though there is no evidence to suggest that these facilities were always used. Free standing, the buildings often incorporated shops for extra income, though this could be counter productive if the patrons bought their cigarettes and confectionery from them, rather than the cinema!

The interior designs were themed, using plenty of plaster ornamentation, striking floor designs for the foyer and public areas and carpet, often with owners monogram woven into it. Pot plants added to the ambience plus a cafe, also open to non patrons. The auditorium seating would be plush, upholstered and of the tip-up variety. The rake of the floor and an absence of pillars supporting the balcony, would ensure uninterrupted vision Heating and ventilating went a stage further than before, introducing air conditioning. Incoming outside air was first washed by water sprays, to remove any contaminants, then passed over a hot water powered heating battery before being fed into the auditorium at higher than head height, avoiding draughts. Vitiated air was extracted through ceiling gratings by electric fans. In hot weather, the heating battery was dispensed with, resulting in cool air being admitted instead. Heating and ventilating of public buildings has always been a challenge. Firstly, the building has to be heated to a comfort level, but when filled, preventing overheating is a problem. Removing the stale(and smoky) air meant introducing a lot of tempered fresh air, without draughts. These new systems, thermostatically controlled, achieved a perfect level of comfort. In fact the air was purer than in the street outside!

The operational side required a high staffing level, with all front of the house personnel in corporate uniforms. The presence of so many staff ensured that

ARCHITECTURE

Astoria, Walton

Trocadero, City

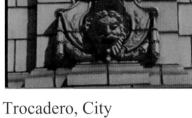

Bankhall

Bedford, Walton

Royal, Breck Road

Regent, Crosby

Royal, Breck Road

Gaumont, Anfield

Empire, Garston

Futurist, Lime Street
Rivoli, Aigburth
Granada, Dovecot
Coliseum, Walton

ARCHITECTURAL STYLES   THE PRINCESS KIRKDALE
Some features of the architect, G. Stanley Lewis ARIBA are shown.

As Mr. Lewis was not one of the main Liverpool cinema architects, his design is worth showing. A picture 28 by 20 foot was produced, with a throw of 130 feet. Wrecked and partly filled in, the narrow screen end, walls and the diverging ceiling ribs show up clearly.

Foyer floor and entrance grating

customers felt specially treated, from being greeted by the commissionaire on the door, to being shown to ones seat. This attention to detail certainly paid off, as they were both popular and profitable, in the decade leading up to the next war.

THE FILMS UP TO 1939

As previously mentioned, the first films were very short and quite crude. The cameras were hand cranked, as were the first projectors. Everything was in black and white, although experiments with colouring by hand were tried. With improvements constantly taking place, films became longer and more ambitious.

Apart from drama and news, serials were introduced, to maintain customer loyalty. "The Perils of Pauline"(1914) always ended an episode where the heroine was in a desparate situation with no means of escape - but she always did, as you found out next week! Programmes developed into a main feature, news, a serial and sometimes a short topical item. A local cameraman would shoot local people-heavy scenes, which would then be shown at the local cinema. "Come and see yourself on the big screen!"

With the length of main pictures increasing, there arose the problem of continuity. The solution was two projectors, changing over seamlessly, by means of synchronising marks on the films. Now that problem had been solved, films could be as long as the director wished!

Subtitles were on the films, accompanied by appropiate music. The author cannot resist referring to a scene from "The Smallest Show On Earth", in which Peter Sellers as the projectionist is showing a silent film, whilst Margaret Rutherford plays the piano. This is what it would have been like in a small hall.

Because the speed of silent projectors was adjustable, a manager could instruct the operator to "speed it up, we've got a queue for the next house". Amazing how fast the horses could go in them days (and the musicians)!

Stars included Rudolf Valentino, smouldering in "The Sheik" and Tom Mix's cowboy adventures. But the home grown film industry was in decline, so much so, that by 1927, the Cinematograph Films Act was passed, which stipulated that a quota of British fims must be screened. This kept "rotten British pictures" on the screen as second features, against the managers wishes, who would have quietly dropped them!

When sound films were introduced in 1929, the death knell was sounded for the small local film makers, as well as the musicians. Synchronised sound on film required expensive equipment, which only the major producers could afford. A lot of silent stars also met their nemesis, as their voices were unsuitable for the new medium. This was also the time of "The Great Depression", restricting studio's budgets. On the plus side, the stage was (literally) set for a new type of entertainment, - the musical.

"All singing, all dancing", it could only be done with sound and the audiences loved it! Paramount Pictures brought out "Paramount on Parade in 1930, as an example of what could now be done. Some household names appeared at this time, John Wayne had his first major role in "The Big Trail"(1930) which flopped! Johnny Weissmuller made his debut in "Tarzan the Ape Man"(1932) There was increasing showing of American films, especially up to 1939. Another introduction from 'across the pond' was colour. Two colour(red and green) films were first produced in 1925, but it was 1932 before a 3 colour camera produced Technicolour. This period also introduced animation in colour. Disney produced shorts, then full length films, such as "Snow White and the Seven Dwarfs (1937), whilst other studios gave birth to the cartoon, as we know it. This was the "Golden Age of Hollywood", although most of their output was in black and white! The last films of the decade included "Gone With The Wind"(1939, colour) and "The Wizard of Oz"(Black and white/colour). Oh, by the way, John Wayne finally had a hit in 1939 with "Stagecoach"!

A typical programme in the 1930's would consist of the main feature, news,adverts, a short feature and a "B" picture. In many cases this was continuous performances all afternoon and evening.(you could stay all day if you wanted!)

But the clouds of war were gathering!

BOOKING FILMS

The first films were just made and copies sold to exhibitors, who were travelling showmen. Once permanent cinemas were established, renting became the norm. The operators could deal direct with the makers, or go through a film booking agency. With the establishment of the circuits and the involvement of American studios, things became a lot harder for the independant cinemas that were left.

Apart from automatically taking the output of a subsidiary studio, a circuit would also agree to show the films produced by certain other companies, on an exclusive basis at first. A selected film was known as the circuit release. This would be exhibited in the following order, firstly town centre, then first run suburban(the supers and premier locations) and finally second run suburban (the lower quality halls). If a film was booked as the ABC release at the Reo, Fazakerley, for example, then the independant Walton Vale Picture House and the Aintree Palace would be automatically barred from hiring it. Only when the circuits had got their mileage out of a film, could the independants have it. They could always rent what was not shown by the circuits(off-circuit films), but these did not always guarantee an audience.

The Cinematograph Films Act of 1927, was previously mentioned. this forced the exhibitors to show a quota of British made pictures. Unfortunately, there were a lot of 'duds' produced while audiences favoured the more sophisticated output from Hollywood. One cinema in London, showed the British films in the morning, whilst the cleaners were in, thus fulfilling its screening quota!

Gaumont and Odeon had separate circuit releases until 1948, when Rank were allowed to combine the two chains.

Norton Street area was where the distributors established their offices, in fact the former Paramount Pictures building survives to this day in Fraser Street, in splendid isolation!

ADVERTISING

This is one big trap for the unwary historian to fall into, whilst trying to find opening or closing dates! Posters were the original favourite form - hoardings full of them! The cinemas carried on what the music halls and theatres did already, with shop windows advertising their programmes(for complimentary

CONSTRUCTION

Plaza, Allerton, steel frame, 1927

Paramount, brick infilling, 1934

The Gaumont Palace, Anfield, 1931. Adverts for the circuit's cinemas on the hoardings.

The Plaza, Crosby, underway in 1938. The local paper is advertising. Using a steel frame enables the auditorium to have unobstructed sight lines, due to no columns.

SUPER CINEMAS

Foyer, Plaza, Crosby

Waiting Room, Granada, Dovecot

Cafe, Reo, Fazakerley

Circle Lounge, Abbey,

Above, Balcony stairs, Astoria, Walton
Right, Circle Lounge, Dingle Gaumont

tickets, of course!). Not all cinemas used newspapers, particularly the smaller independant halls. A 'big' film might justify using the papers, but otherwise local low cost publicity prevailed. Outside every hall would be adverts for the current and future presentations. Patrons could also pick up a wallet sized card listing the next months attractions from the pay box.

Regarding the newspapers, the Liverpool Echo's cinema index provided the most comprehensive list, with additional graphic display blocks for the city centre first runs. The circuits also used a block display to group their cinema presentations in the weekly papers. These also carried a 'whats on' feature reviewing the films (thanks to a supply of free tickets!)

Whilst some of the new cinemas had special opening features in the papers, others just used posters and opened when ready. Likewise for closures, sometimes there might be a paragraph in the paper, but often the adverts simply disappeared from next weeks entertainments page!

FILM CLASSIFICATION

The Cinematograph Act of 1909 gave local councils, not only the power to grant or refuse cinema licences, but to decide if a film was suitable for showing in their area. To try to get some degree of uniformity throughout the country, in 1912 the film industry created an independant, non-governmental body called The British Board of Film Censors. It's remit was to classify films, according to their suitability for specific audiences and to order the removal of any scenes that would offend public decency. There were 43 grounds specified for deletion, including "uneccessary exposure of underclothing" and "over passionate love scenes"! There were only two advisory certificates, 'U' Universal, suitable for children and 'A' Adult. The studio's often had to edit a lot of scenes to get a certificate. In 1927 to get an 'A' certificate, many of Greta Garbo's passionate embraces had to be cut in "Flesh and the Devil" In 1935 a new classification, 'H' for horror film was added, being deemed not suitable for children. The rise of sexual content meant in 1952, the 'X' certificate appeared. This incorporated 'H' films and was the first mandatory age related one. No children under 16 were to view it. This age was raised to 18 in 1970 and an 'AA' certificate added for over 14 year olds. 1982 saw the 'PG' parental guidance, '15' replace '14' and 'X' become '18'. An R18 was created to cover the more explicit films shown in private members only clubs. A '12' appeared in 1989 for theatrical use only, being altered in 2002 to '12A' advisory. This list does not cover video classifications, which are a separate item.

Examples of the change in public morals are "Brief Encounter" of 1945, which was awarded an 'A' because of it's theme of adultery and the 1958 "Carry on Sergeant" which was passed 'U' with no cuts, despite being the first of the 'sex comedies'.

The final decision always rested with the local council, who could pass, order cuts or ban it! Because different councils had different policies, if a film was banned by one then another would pass it, the 'banned' status adding to the films attraction.

SUNDAY OPENING

The Sunday Observance Act of 1780 forbade premises being used for public entertainment or amusement, if persons were being admitted for money. The Theatres Act of 1843 stated that this applied to places registered or licenced for entertainment. But in the 'Bioscope' days, lots of people went to see films on Sunday, as they were shown in demountable fairgrounds, unlicenced halls and even empty shops! Most of the local authorities had no legislation in place to prevent these shows and they flourished until the passing of the Cinematograph Act of 1909 gave them the powers to control exhibiting. The churches had always pressed for Sunday to be kept special, leading to severe restrictions on shop opening and sales, plus limited opening hours for public houses. In Europe, Sundays were more relaxed, with opening allowed of all manner of establishments and this information (with lobbying from the cinema industry) led the government to pass the Sunday Entertainments Act of 1932.

This allowed the local councils to grant licences for Sunday opening as long as a poll showed that the majority of residents were in favour(the last council to allow Sunday cinema on Merseyside was Neston, as late as 1962!). The type of films allowed to be shown had to be 'healthy, wholesome and possibly of an educating character' No 'H' certificates were allowed. A percentage of admission revenue was to go to the Sunday Cinematograph Fund, whose aim was to encourage education by means of film. The Privy Council was the administrator, awarding grants. The British Film Institute was a benificiary of this, being established the following year. Opening hours also were limited so as not to compete with going to church. The end result could be a very bland programme, but at inception, the only alternative was to listen to the wireless (or go to sleep until Monday!). The Sunday Cinema Act of 1972 allowed unconditional licensing to operate and also wound up the cinematograph fund. The Cinemas Act of 1985 repealed four of the previous acts, consolidating the currently relevant parts of them into it. Now it was not an offence under The Sunday Observance Act to show films on a Sunday. A further provision, to ensure that employees had time off, was that no person who had worked the previous six days was allowed to work.

THEATRES AND MOVING PICTURES.

With the growth of the cinemas, the draw of the bioscope rapidly diminished. It was kept as a 'turn' and during the First World War, news from the Front was shown. By the end of the decade, it was used as a 'chaser', to empty the hall ready for the next house. A lot of the music halls themselves were being converted to cinemas, so it gradually faded away. A few theatres were equipped with projection rooms and using a flying screen, were able to show occasional film programmes. the Metropole on Stanley Road, Bootle seemed to alternate between cinema and theatre, whilst the Royal Court in town had a period of film presentations. Even the Central Hall in Renshaw Street had a projection room and the ability to show 35mm. The Empire in Garston still has its screen up in the fly tower, although the last film shown was in 1962.

FIRES IN CINEMAS

The main reason for the 1909 Act was to improve public safety. As the numbers of exhibitors grew, so did the numbers of 'incidents'. The

FIRES IN CINEMAS
A page from the police log, showing typical notifiable incidents

CENTRAL FIRE STATION,
LIVERPOOL,

_____ 192_

Fires in Picture Houses

Swan. 14/11/27. Electric light heating velvet plush canopy
              being used for a rehearsal on stage, canopy
              taken out by fireman and extinguished with
              water.

Victoria. 21/1/28. about 1000 feet of film in bottom spool
              box, film jamming, burnt itself out,
              audience in - no panic.

Garrick. 15/2/28. spool of film, the film being in bad
              condition the sprocket slipped leaving the
              film in the gate lon enough to ignite,
              smouldered away, audience in - no panic.

West Derby. 110/10/27. about 1 yard film jamming in gate,
              extinguished by Operator smothering,
              audience in - no panic.

West Derby. 21/3/28. about 1000 feet in spool box, the
              Operator had just threaded up when it fired,
              supposed cause - overheating or some foreign
              body in gate, the apertures in spool box
              being too large and faulty traps allowed
              the flames to enter spool box, audience
              in - no panic.

Savoy. 2/4/28. wiring and switchboard in vestibule,
              defective electric, extinguished by Brigade
              with Pyrenes. no performance.

Homer. 8/4/28. ventilator over operating room, extinguished
              by Brigade, no performance.

Olympia. 7/8/28. about 1000 feet of film bottom spool box
              in Operating Room, extinguished by staff,
              audience in - no panic.

Victory. 4/9/28. about 2 feet film, Operator neglecting to
              close gate when changing over, extinguished
              by Operator with wet blanket, audience in-
              no panic.

You will see that most fires are in connection with the use of the
nitrate film.

FIRES IN CINEMAS

The auditorium of the Palais de Luxe on Lime Street after the June 1951 fire. The musicians gallery and above the proscenium have been destroyed. The setting back of the screen, due to the steep rake shows up

Salvage operations in the burned-out pit of the Empress Cinema this morning.

Empress, 1955 and The New Premier, also 1955

combination of highly inflammable nitrate film and a heat source meant that any interruption to the passage of film through the projector could often result in the film in the gate bursting into flames. This would have been more alarming to the audience, when the projector was set up among them, causing panic! With the equipment and films located in a fireproof 'box' and physically isolated from the auditorium, any fires in that department should be contained, whilst the hall was evacuated. In addition to the normal doors, the auditorium also had to have emergency exits to outside the building. Upon applying for a licence, the Magistrates would insist that the hall could be emptied within a specified period, more exits having then to be provided to achieve this. All the doors had to open outwards and be fitted with panic bolts on the inside, which if pressed released the door catch. It did not take long for the children to realise that this was an opportunity to get in free, either by getting a mate to open the door or by 'springing' it from the outside. As most of the doors did not open directly into the auditorium, there was no sudden burst of light to give the game away. An eagle-eyed attendant would soon work out the reason that two boys went to the toilet - and ten came back! Some managers took(illegally) revenue protection by securing the doors most at risk, but this eventually led to tragic consequences.

In 1929 at the Glen cinema in Paisley, Scotland, a childrens matinee was in progress when a fire broke out in the projection room. Some of the film had ignited, although there was no danger to the cinema, but somebody saw smoke and shouted "fire". Panic ensued and 72 children lost their lives, most of them being found piled up against a locked fire door. This led to further legislation regarding safety in cinemas, the following year. Fire doors needed to be secured when the building was closed, but proof was then needed that all exits were unimpeded before the public was admitted. At the Bedford, Walton, there was a board with a line of hooks on in the managers office. The padlocks and chains from the panic bolts had to fill every hook, before opening and had to remain there until all the patrons had left.

Another stipulation of the Act was that every premises had to have a designated fireman(usually the commissionaire), who was trained in firefighting. He wore an armband with "Fireman" on it and it was his job to unchain the exits, ensure that the extinguishers, etc, were available for use and be prepared to deal with a fire, either putting it out or trying to contain it until the Fire Brigade arrived. All fires, no matter how small, had to be reported to the magistrates for inclusion in the 'Fires in Cinemas Register'. This could be taken into account when the next licence renewal application was submitted. There were far more fires than the public ever knew about, because most of them were dealt with by the staff. Until the introduction of 'safety film' the most common fires involved film in the projection room igniting by various means. These were usually dealt with by the projectionists themselves, sometimes with help from the fireman. The next most common incident was dropped cigarette ends. These could ignite the carpets and wooden floor beneath, or the seats, which could then smoulder for hours before bursting into flames. It was the cleaners in the morning that would usually encounter such blazes, unless a conflagration had occured during the night and was spotted from outside the building. Although the structure itself was non-combustible, the seating, carpets and woodwork was, which could lead to extensive smoke damage. This risk remained until the banning of smoking in cinemas.

Although the patrons may not yet have realised that a fire had broken out, the staff had to be made aware, so that they could be in position to facilitate the orderly evacuation of the hall. This was achieved by the projection room being instructed to play the 'fire record', a designated piece of music only to be used for this eventuality. The manager could then come on stage to make the announcement (using a microphone that was connected into the sound system assuming that there was still power). Even if the mains electricity failed, the secondary lighting would provide enough illumination to enable the audience to get to safety outside.

With so much electricity involved, fighting a fire could be very dangerous. When the hall was empty, the fireman could isolate the gas and electricity supplies, pending the arrival of the fire brigade, or if unable to access, to tell the firemen the locations. The high voltage outside neon displays had to be fitted with a hook operated 'firemans switch', painted red and located by the fixture, but high enough up to be out of the reach of meddlesome fingers!

THE STAFF

To run any kind of operation requires labour and the cinemas required a lot of it! A super could have fifty people on the books, but what did they all do? At the top was the Manager, who was directly responsible to the owners for the profitability of it. Very much the expert public relations officer, They would be seen smartly dressed in the foyer before the performance, greeting the patrons and sorting out problems ranging from lost children to blocked toilets. Personnel(now human resources) management, which included hiring, firing and rostering was another task. The building also had to be inspected before the public were admitted, especially that all the fire exits were available. The financial responsibilty was also theirs. A good manager could make a lot of difference to the takings by 'theming' the cinema and staff, to complement the film. For example, when "The Ghost Train" was being shown at the Trocadero (Gaumont), Camden Street, the foyer was decorated to resemble a railway booking hall.

There could be assistant managers, then the cashier, commissionaire(who you never gave lip to, as he had the power of admission!), usherettes, even page boys.

The usherettes had long days, starting with managers parade, at which your uniform had to be immaculate, brass buttons polished and no ladders in your stockings! No high heels or excessive makeup either. The doors would open and you would each stand at a gangway, as it filled up passing the people along to the next one by torch. No talking to each other or sitting down was allowed. After about two hours, there was a short tea break, then back on duty until an hours meal break(if conditions allowed). The programme generally finished at 10.30, which meant at least ten hours on your feet. and it was a six day working week! The page boys were under the control of the commissionaire and their duties were to show the customers to their seats, by which there was the opportunity for tips! They were also 'on parade' where the manager would pay special attention to the cleanliness of their hands! Then there were the projectionists, who apart from showing films, did bulb changing and in the smaller halls, seat repairs, painting, boiler stoking, plus whatever else that the manager wanted doing. There would be a chief and up to several others in a seniority order. Again the hours were long, but this time

FILM TRANSPORT SERVICES

Due to restrictions on the movement of nitrate film by public carriers, the distributors set up the above company to service the cinemas.

As a graphic illustration as to how inflammable the film was, one of the vans had just loaded up in Norton Street on the 18 August 1947. It turned into London Road and went on fire. Scorched shopfronts, cracked windows and a written off van!

Bag shrink wrapped through glass!!

CIRCUIT RELEASES

The managers were advised in advance by their company's film booking department. This is a typical ABC notice, sent to the Carlton, Tuebrook, in 1962. The childrens Saturday films are listed at the bottom.

ASSOCIATED BRITISH CINEMAS, LTD.

30-31, GOLDEN SQUARE, LONDON, W.1.

MANAGER'S ADVANCE PROGRAMME ADVICE

| Town | TUEBROOK | Theatre | CARLTON |
| Programme for P9181/10M/Form 410/662 | FIVE | days commencing | 24.12.62.(Closed Xmas Day) |

TITLE etc.	Cert.	Description	Regd. No.	Length	Renter
"THE PASSWORD IS COURAGE" Dirk Bogarde Maria Perschy Alfred Lynch	U		BR/E. 27827	116	MGM.
SHARES		FIRST FEATURE BRITISH QUOTA			
"SERENA" Honor Blackman Patrick Holt	U		BR/E. 27826	61	BUTCHER
FLAT		SUPPORTNG PROGRAMME BRITISH QUOTA			
NEWS.	-	Topical SUPPORTING PROGRAMME BRITISH QUOTA		7	WARNER PATHE
				184 Mins.	

"SERENA" TO RECEIVE 25% OF ALL ADVERTISING.

Typed by _____

Checked by ENL/VG

Kindly send your comments immediately, otherwise no alteration can be considered.

FILM BOOKING DEPARTMENT.

Date...... 6 - NOV 1962 ...... Signature...... E.N. LAWRANCE.

N.B.—This form to be retained by the Manager for reference.

SATURDAY DECEMBER	29th. 1962	MINUTES	
RIP VAN WINKLE	COMEDY. JAMIE UYS	55	N.RLM
ROVER MAKES GOOD	ADVENTURE STORY	16	C.F.F.
MIGHTY MOUSE IN WITCH'S CAT	(Tech) MIGHTY MOUSE CARTOON	6	FOX
ROUND TRIP TO MARS (Tech)	WOODY WOODPECKER CARTOON	6	RANK
THE BATMAN Ep.8	SERIAL	17	B.L.C.

The films are listed with the classification, running time (in minutes) and the distributor/studio. "Shares" meant it was also shown concurrently at other ABC first run suburban houses. "Flat" meant that it is shown in widescreen not Cinemascope. Note that the British Quota is still in operation (see text).
Many times, the distributors stated how the films were to be advertised, like "Serena", above.
Using the running times, the programme could then be made up and the showing times advertised.
With the short 'ABC Minors' films, all those little bits of arc carbons could be used up!

Above is a page from the projectionists log book at the Derby Cinema, March 1959. The film, running time, renter and condition of the print are shown.

Loads of memos from head office, this one about the volume levels to be used for maximum effect when screening the latest Cliff Richard film "The Young Ones"

ASSOCIATED BRITISH CINEMAS LTD.
30-31 Golden Square, London, W.1.

FROM: N. Mole

Our Ref. NM/MAF

TO: All Theatre Managers

Your Ref.

27th December, 1961.

When "THE YOUNG ONES" starring Cliff Richard is played at your theatre will you please comply with the following instructions:-

Rehearse reel No. 1 at normal fader setting until you come to the first dialogue sequence, which is an interior shot of Cliff Richard talking to Robert Morley, on this dialogue adjust the fader to give a good clear reproduction. When playing the remainder of the film the music sequences will at first appear to you to be louder than necessary. This is intended by the Producers as the type of sound being reproduced is required to be played above normal level, all sound variations are catered for in the recording. It could be that this film will be enthusiastically received by teenage audiences, in which case excessive audience noise will be created. Should this occur then you must arrange to increase sound volume to compensate this ambient noise.

N.MOLE.
Sound and Projection Engineer.

c.c. District Engineer.

Running Time	TITLE AND STARS		Cat.	SCREENING TIMES			
				1st	2nd	3rd	4th
	SUNDAY			WEEKDAYS			
5	Houselights	6.15			4.30	7.27	
30	THE PIPELINERS	6.20	U		4.35	7.32	
7	S A L E S .	6.50			5.05	8.02	
14	R.S.S. & Trailers	4.00 6.57			55.12	8.09	
2.01	WINNING	4.14 7.11	A		5.26	8.23	
2.57	STAFF PARADE SUNDAY 3.30 Weekdays 4.15 DOORS 3.45 " 4.15 THE QUEEN 9.12 " 10.24						

TIME SHEET   Commencing 10/5/70

Theatre LIVERPOOL HIPPODROME   Town

Theatre No. 7

SPECIAL NOTES

DOORS OPEN _____   QUEEN _____

Signed E. Bennison MIC
Manager.

This shows the timing of the show, in this case the last week of the Royal Hippodrome's life.

ADVERTISING
Some fine poster displays resulted, plus the press and handbills.

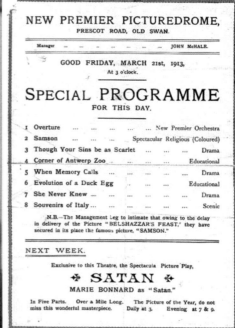

NEW PREMIER PICTUREDROME,
PRESCOT ROAD, OLD SWAN.

Manager ... ... JOHN McHALE.

GOOD FRIDAY, MARCH 21st, 1913,
At 3 o'clock.

SPECIAL PROGRAMME
FOR THIS DAY.

1	Overture	... New Premier Orchestra	
2	Samson	Spectacular Religious (Coloured)	
3	Though Your Sins be as Scarlet	...	Drama
4	Corner of Antwerp Zoo	...	Educational
5	When Memory Calls	...	Drama
6	Evolution of a Duck Egg	...	Educational
7	She Never Knew	...	Drama
8	Souvenirs of Italy	...	Scenic

N.B.—The Management beg to intimate that owing to the delay in delivery of the Picture "BELSHAZZAR'S FEAST," they have secured in its place the famous picture, "SAMSON."

NEXT WEEK.

Exclusive to this Theatre, the Spectacular Picture Play,

✤ SATAN ✤

MARIE BONNARD as "Satan."

In Five Parts.   Over a Mile Long.   The Picture of the Year, do not miss this wonderful masterpiece.   Daily at 3.   Evening at 7 & 9.

Early handbill, giving the type of film as well.

Monthly pocket film listings

Weekly free pass for posters in shop

★ For All That Is Best In Cinemagoing Visit Your Local A.B.C. Cinema

Astoria Walton ★ Commodore Bankhall ★ Gainsborough Bootle ★ Regal Litherland ★ Victory Walton

they were isolated from the other staff. If the chief was youngish, the only way for a second to get promoted would be to apply for the chiefs vacancy at another cinema in the chain. The extra money would more than compensate for increased travelling and the hours were better too. Projectionists were sometimes given the chance to move to the management side but electrical engineering did not always convert into good public relations. One of the least popular projectionists chores was to have to put a ladder up to the projection ports, to clean condensation or tobacco film off the glass! There was a common driving force to give the best possible show, including perfect changeovers. Because of the hours worked, a lot of socialising was with other cinema staff and the projectionists tended to meet others of the same ilk from other cinemas. Some of them also liked to see other boxes, but circuit rivalry often meant that, for example, a Rank manager would not let an ABC projectionist see his box.

Lastly there were cleaners and perhaps a car park attendant. Cleaning was an endless task, especially after a childrens matinee! All the seat back ashtrays also had to be emptied and cleaned and there could be hundreds of them! A lot of the later buildings had 'hygienic' floor coverings(posh lino), which could just be mopped, but where there was strips of carpet between the seat rows it was a lot more labour intensive. The cleaners were the first employees in the morning to enter the premises and found, not that infrequently, fires caused by smouldering cigarettes, that patrons had improperly disposed of the previous evening. Although the main structure of the building was non-combustible, the seats were mounted on a wooden floor and there were the upholstered wood seat panels as well. Extra hours could often be worked as an usherette, especially the Saturday morning childrens show.

One of the large supers might employ a handyman, one of whose jobs would be to stoke the heating boiler. This would be located in a cellar and have a storage area with a chute from outside, for coke deliveries. First job of the morning would be to open up the draught controls, give it a good riddling and de-clinker the firebed. Once it was burning brightly, fresh coke would be added, the ashpits emptied and the air intakes set to the day position. If there was a circulating pump, this would be started, so as to get the hall warmed up. The ash would have to be carried in buckets upstairs, to the bins. Periodically, the boiler flues would have to be cleaned with a long scraper and brush. As if this was not bad enough, the air could be filled with choking coke fumes! You may well ask, why not use gas? Until North Sea Gas and the gas grid came along, coal gas was produced from local gasworks. As there was a limit to the amount that could be produced, there were restrictions on its commercial use. That is why all the public buildings and schools used coke, a cheap by-product of making coal gas. In the 1950's the availability of cheap heating oil led to the conversion/replacement of boilers and automatic controls replaced manual labour. Due to lack of capital investment, a lot of cinemas spent all their active lives heated by coke.

The size and status of the hall governed the amount of staff and how specific the jobs were. One thing was common, the hours were long and anti-social, but it was a job. A lot of the staff had a love for the cinema, which helped them to stay the course.

THE PROJECTION ROOM

Few cinemagoers, on entering the auditorium, would look towards the rear wall. Those that did, would see a number of small glass windows, near the ceiling. if you were really lucky, then a face might appear momentarily at one of them, but what lay behind? What follows is a simplified description of the 'box' in the 'golden age' of the cinema.

The 1909 Act required that the projection equipment be completely isolated from the audience in a fire resisting enclosure (or box) This meant that the construction was usually of brick and reinforced concrete. the Act also stated that film rewinding must be done in a separate room. That meant a minimum of two fireproofed rooms. The constant enemy here is fire, due to the inflammable nature of the filmstock then in use. Heavy, self closing, steel firedoors were used to isolate the rooms and any corridor that connected them. Access to the projection suite was usually from a corridor at the rear of the balcony (or stalls if a stadium type) One or two had entrance from outside only. The stairs would be either a stone flight or a cast iron spiral type, to save space. At the head, the first steel door would be reached, leading to a passage with similar doors off, all signed. In the Rewind Room, the film would be transferred to the cinemas reels, using a hand operated geared winder on a bench. The film would be examined and a note made of its condition. Any tears would be cut out and the film spliced back together using film cement. The reels were then placed into individually numbered, closed steel containers in a rack in the projection room. Any making up of programmes, trailers, etc, would also be done in here. From 1952, the safer and more robust cellulose triacetate film base was introduced and this was superceded by polyester, from the early 1990's. The original nitrate film was also liable to decomposition over time.

Projection rooms varied in size greatly. Some were hardly bigger than the projectors, while others (in the later cinemas especially) were as big as a mini cinema! The projecting and viewing ports were of plate glass with steel shutters running in vertical guides, to be dropped in case of fire. Centre stage were always the projectors themselves. Two was normal, but a large city centre cinema could have an extra one to cover breakdowns. The basic parts consisted of a heavy stand, the mechanism itself and a lamp housing. As most rooms were higher than the centre of the screen, the projector had to be tilted downwards, so that the beam would illuminate the screen, which would also have to be set back at the same angle otherwise part of the picture would be out of focus. Some of the angles could be so steep that part of the take up spool case would be in a slot cut out of the floor! Excessive rake would also mean that the first few front row patrons would get a distorted picture. The mechanism consisted of a top feed spool, the 'gate' where the frame rested whilst being projected, and a lower take up spool. Once 'laced up' the film path would be from the top spool box, through a narrow slit(fire stop), into the gate, past the optical sound head and via another slit onto the take up spool. If there was magnetic sound, the head would be before the gate. A safety shutter on the lamp side of the gate was held open as long as the mechanism was running and instantly cut the light if it stopped or slowed down, to stop the film burning out in the intense heat. The lamphouse contained two carbon rods and a reflector to focus the intense light on the

PROJECTION ROOMS

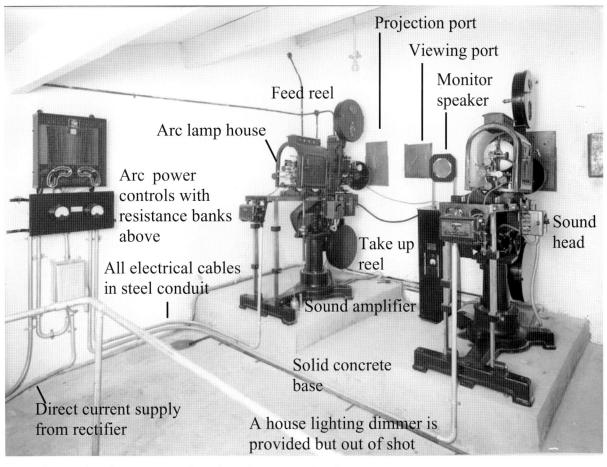

Projection port

Viewing port

Monitor speaker

Feed reel

Arc lamp house

Arc power controls with resistance banks above

All electrical cables in steel conduit

Take up reel

Sound head

Sound amplifier

Direct current supply from rectifier

Solid concrete base

A house lighting dimmer is provided but out of shot

Basic projection room showing layout. The lamp cases are open backed, showing the arc reflector. Later cases were enclosed with vent

Spotlight with coloured filters

Stage lighting board

Arc power controls

Note the bigger lamp cases as more light was needed and the rake on the projectors. The screen was set back to the same angle.

Small halls tended to have only the basic items, as above. The larger ones had far bigger suites and had a greater range of fittings. Both pictures from 1937.

PROJECTION ROOMS continued

This is the carbon arc assembly, inside the lamp house. The positive carbon has a pointed tip and is on the left. Behind it is the reflector to give a parallel, even beam of light to the condenser lens and then film gate.

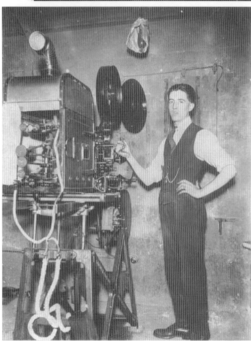

Left, Homer, Gt. Homer St. Above, 3 projectors, Cinerama, Abbey Wavertree.

Above, Mayfair, Aigburth
Right, Princess, Kirkdale

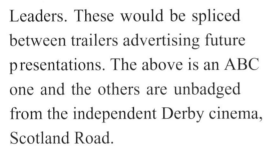

Leaders. These would be spliced between trailers advertising future presentations. The above is an ABC one and the others are unbadged from the independent Derby cinema, Scotland Road.

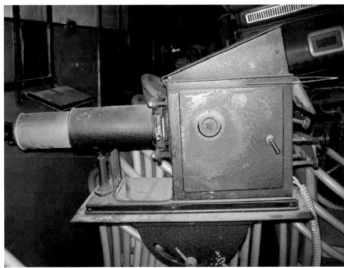

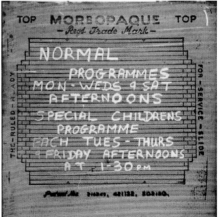

A lot of larger cinemas also had an arc slide projector, which was used for messages on screen. Slides were of glass and were either bought ready made, or blanks to 'scratch-em yourself'. The grid does not show on the screen. These are from the Majestic, Daulby Street

TECHNICAL BITS

Westar projector, 2000ft reels

Projector gate.Inspection light is top left, spring loaded gate in the middle.

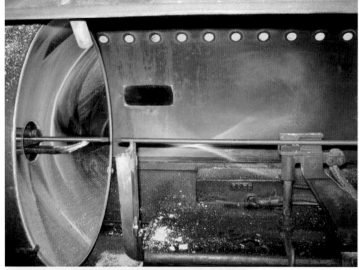

Lamphouse with carbons and the arc through dark green glass crater in right (+) tip on left(-)

Cinemascope anamorphic lens, showing vertical stretching of image, as the frames of film would be. When projected, the lens would compress the picture to normal vertically, increasing the width to produce widescreen.

SECONDARY LIGHTING

50 volt battery and control unit

HEATING - Gas converted coke boilers in the London Road Odeon

Above, 1931, 110 volt control unit. The large wheel operates a resistance for 'floating' the battery across the load.

Good old gas light

VENTILATION

Plant room at the London Road Odeon
Exhaust fan, Bootle Gaumont, + dud seats

DIRECT CURRENT SUPPLY

Motor-generator set, open cage dynamo on left direct coupled to three phase AC motor.
Mercury arc rectifier, 'arms' contain carbon anodes.

Above,Arc control unit, switchable resistances on right
Above right, solid state rectifiers by projectors, ABC Southport
To provide a steady direct current for the projection arcs from the alternating current mains, firstly came the motor-generator set. From the 1930's, mercury arc rectifiers appeared. With no moving parts they were more efficient, but had to have a load on them at all times, so a 'shunt' resistance was used(not efficient). Lastly diode or solid state, which is still used today. These are compact, as seen above.
The arc must have a resistance in series with it, which is variable for matching output. Voltage is 20-60 and amps 30-100 to suit hall size.

gate. The carbons were copper coated to improve conductivity and there was a negative and a thicker positive one. Most of the light was generated from the positive, (the tip of which formed a crater) which would burn away quicker. For interest, the arc temperature is about 3,600 degrees Centigrade and can only be viewed through a very dark filter, due to the intensity and the amount of ultra violet rays produced. The arc was started by briefly touching the rods together, then retracting them to a preset gap. Originally the rods had to be hand fed, but it was quickly mechanised. The main thing to make sure of was that the rods were long enough to last the reel. Short bits were used up on the childrens films. A 'snuffer' which interrupted the arc was used for extinguishing. Fumes were safely removed by ducts leading vertically outside, hence the 'stove pipes' protruding from the box roof. The arc itself could be viewed through a dark green window at the side. The 'Xenon' high pressure discharge bulb gradually replaced the arc and allowed hours of film to be shown at a time. They are expensive but require no attention and neither do they produce fumes, just heat.

Larger halls had an arc lantern for showing glass slides of advertisements or messages.

The standard spool holds 2000 feet of film and lasts about twenty minutes. For a film longer than this, it must be in parts which are shown alternately on each projector. As previously mentioned, the reels of film are stored in sequentially numbered fireproof boxes, giving the running order. Each film leader has a countdown of numbers to 3. The second projector is laced up with the 'start' frame in the gate. When the reel is nearing its end on the first projector, a white circle appears briefly in the top right hand corner of the film. (look out for this on the telly!) This is the cue to start the second projector with the safety shutter down. When a second cue dot is shown, the shutter is raised whilst the first one is dropped and the sound is also switched over. There are devices that did all the actions, needing only one lever or switch to operate. The 'shown' reel is put back in its case for rewinding (and woe betide anyone that forgot one!).

Other equipment would consist of dimmers for the house and stage lights, amplifiers,with a monitor speaker, a record deck for interval music and the arc control gear consisting of a number of resistances that could be switched in or out of series with the arc, controlling its intensity. There would also be controls for altering the screen masking. The curtains were also controlled from here, either by a hand operated windlass or electrically. At the rear of the hall were two push buttons which an usherette could use to have the sound level raised or lowered. These operated an indicator panel in the box. An internal telephone connected to other parts of the building. Near the record deck would be the fire record. This was played to warn the staff, without the customers being aware that anything was wrong. There always had to be an alternative way out, in case of emergency. In a lot of cases this was simply a door leading to a section of flat roof behind the top of the facade but it also could be a fixed escape ladder.

Behind another door would be the rectifier room. The first cinemas had the problem that the public electricity supply was alternating current, but the arc required the direct variety. The solution was to use a three phase motor (because these ran at a constant speed irrespective of load) directly coupled to a dynamo. These motor generating sets were mounted on mats, to reduce the noise, and although replacement rectifiers were more efficient, many of them were in use for the whole life of the cinema. As long as the commutators and brush gear were maintained plus the bearings kept well greased, they were extremely reliable. The next generation of rectifier was the mercury arc. Housed in a metal case, when seen in operation it looked like something out of science fiction. A large glass bulb, widest at the top, had glass arms fused into it at a lower level. Wires led to carbon electrodes inside the arms and the bottom of the bulb held a pool of mercury. This worked on the principle that carbon produced few electrons, while mercury would produce many. As electricity is a stream of electrons, they could only pass in one direction, creating direct current.. Under load, the bulb glowed with a greenish blue light and coils of plasma roiled about, as if trying to escape! This was very efficient, having no moving parts and nothing to wear out. Finally, solid state or diode rectifiers were introduced and are still used today. Housed in a neat metal cabinet, they could be located next to the projector. The arc current required would be between 30 to 60 volts and the current up to 100 amps. The actual figures would depend on the amount of light required, and the length of throw to the screen.

For cinemas that had electric secondary lighting, there was the battery room. Racks contained rows of lead-acid accumulators, connected in series, to give the required voltage, which was governed by the size of the building. A small hall might only need a 24 volt supply, but for a very large one it could be 110. The battery was 'floated', ie; direct current from a rectified mains supply was fed across the battery output to power the lighting. In the event of a mains failure, the load would then be supplied from the battery without interruption. The control unit would be regulated to give very slightly more current than was used, in order to keep a full charge. There was also provision for re-charging after use. A regular job would be topping the cells up with distilled water and checking the strength of the acid/water solution.

While this chapter only gives a general account of 'behind the scenes', it should at least give the reader some idea about what was happening in a part of the cinema that very few people ever saw. The only other room, sometimes provided, would contain a sink and toilet, so that the projection suite was self contained.

A modern 'box' contains just one projector, the whole film programme on a giant reel and an assortment of computerised panels. One projectionist can control multiple showings, unlike the labour intensive system just described. Modern film is made of polyester which will not break, in fact if it jams the projector can be pulled over! It is, more importantly, stable and not inflammable like the old cellulose nitrate films were, though it will melt!

At the present time, digital projection is taking over. This is simply a powerful digital projector fed from a portable hard drive, which contains the entire programme. The entire show can be controlled from anywhere, with full automation of lights and curtains. Soon, most films will only be available in a digital format and the high cost and limited life of film prints will be avoided.

CHILDRENS CLUBS

Most cinemas hosted a childrens matinee on a Saturday. Usually in the morning, but it could be in the afternoon, where the adult programme was only shown in the evening. The circuits created 'clubs' to encourage loyalty, hence the "ABC Minors", "Gaumont British Junior Club" and "Granadiers" (with the name of the theatre prefixed). Essoldo only had childrens shows where there was a demand(and a profit!) ABC started it's clubs in October 1945 to compete with the others and they lasted until 1980. Club badges could be bought, the ABC ones glowed in the dark! Loyalty treats included free admission and a small bag of sweets on your birthday, plus competitions on stage such as Yo-yo's and Hula Hoops. Programmes consisted of cartoons, a short feature, the serial and the main picture, usually an old cowboy one in black and white. At the Bedford in the late 1950's the National Anthem was played first, the film showing a very young Queen, trooping the colour - in colour! Before the show started at the Astoria, the manager(or a press-ganged assistant!) would come on the stage to make any announcements, ask for birthdays and then cue the club song, the words on screen complete with bouncing ball. Being an ex- ABC Minor, their song is still going round in my head, decades later;

"We are the boys and girls well known as
Minors of the ABC
And every Saturday all line up
To see the films we like and shout aloud with glee
We like to laugh and have a sing-song
Just a happy crowd are we
We're all pals together
We're minors of the ABC"   To the tune of "Blaze Away"

There then followed cartoons, a short feature such as Pathe's "Look at Life" and then the serial. A lot of these were twenty years old, or more, "Republic" and"RKO" comes to mind as two of the main producers of them.
At the end of every episode, the hero/heroine would be in a certain death situation, but the start of next week's instalment would have an additional scene slipped in to show a last second escape! "Flash Gordon" and "Sherlock Holmes" are two that I can remember. The main picture tended to be old 'B' movies, westerns, but sometimes something different - and in colour! Walt Disneys "Fantasia" was shown at a Bedford matinee in 1958(but it was over running, so they cut the last reel and brought the house lights up!) "The Adventures of Robin Hood" also in colour, was on the bill at the ABC Astoria one week in 1962.
Seating policy varied. At the Bedford, you could sit wherever you wanted in the stalls, but at the Astoria, the cleaners acted as the usherettes and starting at the back stalls, directed the stream of children to fill the rows of seats with military precision! The front stalls toilets had a rope tied across the door handles, putting them out of use. No doubt that the cleaners were keeping mess to the minimum! Under cover of darkness, all kinds of mischief was practiced. Apple cores, gobstoppers, sweets and chewing gum were popular missiles to be launched at the front rows. Quite a few girls ended up with short hair after the gum found its mark! Perhaps the ultimate weapon was a

sucked out "Jubbly". These were affordable(3d in the fifties) triangular frozen orange drinks in a cardboard outer. When all the orange had been sucked out, the remaining ice was launched forwards. To be hit by one had the same effect as a half-brick! Throwing objects through the projector beam was another popular trick. Balls of paper were the favourite, though on one occasion a shoe defied gravity! If the unfortunate child could not recover it, the parents not being amused would be an understatement! Butlins rewarded customers children with free tickets to a film show. In 1965, one was held at the New Regent, Prescot Road, Old Swan. The Beavers were put in the stalls, whilst the ABC Minors, whose show it was, occupied the balcony. Any Beaver unfortunate enough to sit below was subjected to a rain of assorted rubbish, as the Minors showed their displeasure to the 'invaders'.

Keeping order could be a problem. In the Astoria, cleaners torches were directed on suspected miscreants, who could then be thrown out! A lot of the main features were much worn and spliced prints, film breaks being quite common. The picture would freeze for a split second and then erupt into a brown roiling mess, before the safety shutter could be dropped. The resulting darkness was not appreciated, a chant of "oooh, oooh, oooh" would start, with stamped accompaniment (choking on the dust from the carpets!) This would bring the manager on stage to threaten total eviction, but often the film would restart, leaving him trying to compete with a twenty foot high cowboy behind!

Going to the toilet could also be a problem if you were in the middle of a row and the odd child that could not hold it would just 'let it go' where they were, often changing seats afterwards to avoid detection! The attendants would retaliate by spraying disinfectant from a 'Flit' type gun over the audience. This was common at the Queens in Walton Road for example, one of the children remarking that the pinhead sized droplets on your skin would sting.

Throughout the 1960's and '70's, the cinema closures continued unabated. Competitition appeared in the form of Saturday morning childrens television and by 1978, there were only 300 Saturday matinees left across the country.
In 1980, the ABC Minors were no longer "all pals together" and Rank disbanded the Super Saturday Club the following year, thus bringing to an end another piece of social history. No more could parents get some peace on a Saturday by giving their little darlings a shilling to go to the pictures(6d to get in, 6d for an ice cream (or 2 Jubbly's!) to consume or throw at the contestants on stage twisting balloons!)

Perhaps the most amazing thing is that small children would go on their own, sometimes walking quite a long way. Parents gaily sent their offspring out, not worrying that something horrible might happen to them.

After all, though, it was a different world back then.

Just for devilment, here is the Odeon song, noble and patriotic stuff.

"We come along on a Saturday morning, greeting everybody with a smile
We come along on a Saturday morning, knowing it's all worthwhile
As members of the Odeon Club, we all intend to be
Good citizens when we grow up and Champions of the Free"

PROMOTIONS
Three examples of displays by staff in conjunction with films.

Nautical flavour at the Queens, South Road, Waterloo for the 1943 film "San Demetrio London"

No, this has not escaped from a train book! The Trocadero, later Gaumont in Camden Street was decorated to resemble a railway booking hall for "The Ghost Train" The style is Great Western Railway but a sign at the rear proclaims Mersey Railway!

This is all Greek to me! "Hercules Unchained" is this 1960 display. The scooter is being pulled by the bored looking slaves to save petrol and where is his helmet? Did the Ancient Greeks have scooters then? This is suspect!

CHILDRENS CLUBS

Full house at the Plaza, Widnes in 1939

Sixpence, not the adult prices at the Hippodrome in 1966

Clockwise, Astoria 1949, Gainsboro' 1956, Bootle Gaumont 1956, Astoria 1962

New Cinema's Boys' And Girls' Club Opens

Children win Yo - Yo prizes at Astoria

So popular that annuals were produced. Badges could be bought, making you a member. The three main circuit ones are shown. ABC issued several styles over time, this 1961 example glowed in the dark!

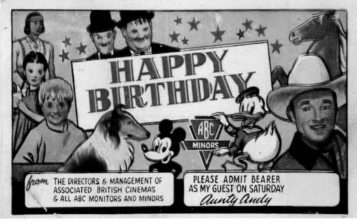

Birthday card, ice creams and a picture of the dreaded Jubbly!

THE BOYS' AND GIRLS' CLUB

Meets Every Saturday Morning at 11 a.m.

Specially Selected Film Programmes and Club Activities

THE CHILDRENS FILM FOUNDATION

This was created in 1951, to provide quality films for the childrens matinees. After the Second World War, several educationalists were raising objections as to the films being screened for children. Entry prices had to be kept to pocket money levels, but a lot of enterprising managers realised that the youngsters were happy with films and serials that were as much as twenty years old(and thus very cheap to hire!) Following the Wheare Report of 1950, into juvenile cinema-going, this was the answer. Funding was via the British Film Production Fund(or 'Eady Levy'), a voluntary levy taken from all cinema ticket prices, with some 5% destined for the CFF.

In 1951, this gave a production budget of some £60,000. Even allowing for the fact that most films lasted less than an hour and were shot in less than a fortnight, this was incredibily low. The early offerings were nearly all shot in black and white and followed the CFF template of "clean, healthy ,intelligent adventure without sensationalism, unhealthy excitement or vulgarity". Fortunately for this country, the CFF children were utterly brave and resourceful, the fact that the villains were painfully thick working class types, helped them as well. England was under threat from cockney-accented criminals, engaged in jewel thieving, low-grade spying and almost non-violent bank robberies! The films would always end with the police arriving in their bell-clanging Wolseley's as the baddies floundered in a convenient duck pond! An inspector would tell the children that "they were a credit to their nation" and roll closing credits! With such a 'jolly super time being had by all', it was only natural that Enid Blyton's first "Famous Five" film was made by the CFF.

By 1963, there was enough money to allow for colour filming on location, but after a survey revealed that 'cops and robbers' were losing their appeal, the bias was on "childrens strong instinct for fair play and a pronounced sympathy for the underdog". The successes of the 1960's steadily increased their budget, allowing global locations to be used, but then ITV launched "Zokko", the first Saturday morning childrens television show. "Tiswas" and the BBC's "Multi -coloured Swap Shop" followed, the CFF retaliating by going all colour(colour TV's were not in the majority until 1977).There were less spiffing adventures and more dramas that captured a now lost England of Spangles and Ford Cortinas.

But this was the era of cinema closures and the abolition of childrens shows. Despite some good productions, the number of screens were shrinking fast. The abolition of the "Eady Levy" in 1985 dealt it a mortal blow and production ceased in 1987/8(so did the British sex comedy!) As the Childrens Film and Television Foundation it still exists, but only as an advisory body. Although BBC Television was screening CFF films into the 1980's, most of them are just now fading memories from an innocent childhood.

The adult actors were employed at minimum Equity rates, the children, being subject to restrictions in terms of union and educational legislation, were from the Italia Conti Stage School. The fact that they had all been trained in the art of clear theatre speaking, accounted for their precise diction. Some of the children went on to be stars in their own right. to give just a few;
"Adventure in the Hopfields" (1954) with Mandy Miller (you remember, she

sang "Nelly the Elephant"!)
"Go Cart Go" (1963) featured Dennis Waterman (no he didn't sing the theme tune!)
"Calamity the Cow" (1967) had a young Phil Collins
"Anoop and the Elephant" (1972) Linda Robson and Phil Daniels
"The Boy With Two Heads" (1974) Lesley Ash

THE 1940'S - WAR, PEACE AND QUEUE THIS SIDE

When war was declared, all cinemas were closed by Government decree. This was quickly rescinded and by 18 September most were open again, it being realised how important they were to public morale. Most experienced a drop in takings, but they continued to provide a temporary escape from the deprivations of the conflict. Some cinemas, indeed, had regular full houses as the only other source of entertainment was the wireless. Programmes ended early at about 9pm and continued during bombing raids. A slide would be flashed onto the screen stating "An air raid is now in progress and those who wish to leave are asked to do so calmly". Few did, as people thought that they were safer inside, than playing 'Russian Roulette' with falling bombs, while trying to get to a shelter. Patrons were allowed to remain after the show, until the 'all clear' was given. To keep spirits up, music or the organ was played. Over 300 cinemas across the country were destroyed and Merseyside did not escape unscathed. The Broadway on Stanley Road, Bootle had the auditorium destroyed in the blitz of May 1941 and the New Adelphi in Christian Street, off Islington, also met its end at the same time. The Palais de Luxe on Lime Street was also damaged, but re-opened after a month. The Ritz in Birkenhead suffered the worst incident, when, on the 21 December 1940 a bomb penetrated the roof and exploded in the auditorium. A lot of patrons were still in there, waiting for the raid to end, resulting in over a hundred casualties including fatalities. As if for good measure, a bomb outside shattered the rear wall as well! The Avenue cinema was also destroyed on March 12 1941, during one of the heaviest raids.
Staffing levels suffered, due to call ups, although projectionists were later 'reserved occupations'. Women again filled jobs that normally men would do, including projecting films, but unlike post World War 1, they did not have to give them up at the end of hostilities.
Because America was neutral at first, there was a good supply of Hollywoods prodigious output. Then the American film industry used its might to further the war effort, producing government propaganda and a glut of war films like "The Maltese Falcon", which were always biased in favour of the Allies. The British industry did the same, although some ordinary films continued to be made. Perhaps one of the most memorable offerings, to lighten 'our darkest hour' was "Casablanca" (1942) "Play it again, Sam" became a catchphrase and Humphrey Bogart was a household name. Tarzan kept on swinging about the jungle, throughout the whole decade. There was also the "Road to ...." series. Basil Rathbone was Sherlock Holmes in Universal's series of adventures(1942+) "Bambi"(1942) and the fantasy "The Thief of Bagdad"(1940) were in colour.
When peace finally returned, it was to a weary and battered Britain. Rationing continued and there were fuel shortages, which led to restrictions on the hours that cinemas could open. The halls themselves showed the results of

five years of deferred maintainance and decoration. Due to Ministry of Supply restrictions, permission to repair or rebuild could take years to obtain. In 1946, cinema admissions hit a record high of 1635 million, then started to decline. Post war films included David Leans atmospheric Dickens duo, "Great Expectations"(1946) and "Oliver Twist"(1947). The short lived Ealing studios gave us "Passport to Pimlico", "Whiskey Galore" and "Kind Hearts and Coronets"(all 1949). To round it all off, Cecil B. DeMille's first biblical epic "Samson and Delilah"(1949). With a limitation on the number of prints available of new films, exhibitors resorted to putting two previously 'run' ones together as a 'double bill'. Unless it was a 'must see again', this did no favours for ticket sales, but did keep the cinemas open.

The motion picture industry had blossomed, despite two world wars, but now a far more deadly threat was now gathering strength in the wings.

THE 1950'S - INNOVATION AND CONSOLIDATION

Shortly before the war, the BBC had launched the country's first television service, only for it to be abruptly suspended for the period of hostilities. When it returned to the airwaves, there was limited broadcasting time and the programmes were largely studio based. Wartime technology advances were then incorporated, so that by 1953, the Coronation of Queen Elizabeth the second was televised in its entirety as an outside broadcast. Televisions at the time were large pieces of furniture with a ten or twelve inch screen. To make the picture bigger, an oil-filled magnifiying lens would be placed in front of it(this also magnified the scanning lines!) But it was in the comfort of your living room! Thus millions saw the Coronation in real-time black and white and were converted to the new medium.

In the United States, television was more developed and widespread, with multiple channels. There was already a war between Hollywood and the 'box in the corner'. The movie moguls decided to develop the things that TV could not provide, namely colour and widescreen. More and more films were made in colour(that was the easy bit) but one type of widescreen demanded that the image was compressed horizontally on the film, so that when shown through a special (anamorphic) lens it became wider again. This very simple description was the basis of "Cinemascope". Coupled with this was 'magnetic, stereophonic sound', replacing the mono optical soundtrack. Cinemas would have to invest in a much larger new screen, with adjustable top, bottom and side masking(so ordinary films could still be shown), then there was the cost or rental of the new sound system. In some cases, projector lamp houses would have to be replaced to cope with the larger screen area. Another innovation was 3D, where the audience wore spectacles consisting of a red and a green filter. Both projectors were used, synchronised, showing slightly different angles of the same print. Problems began with breakdowns resulting from running the projectors continuously, instead of alternately. Worse still, taking frames out of either print destroyed the effect and could even make the patrons feel ill! There was also a lack of 3D films, so it quietly faded away. "Vistavision" was Paramounts higher resolution wide screen system, shooting on to a larger negative to make a finer grained print. whilst no special lens was required, it became obsolete with the development of finer grained film. Todd-AO was an extreme high definition widescreen format using 70mm film. with 6 magnetic soundtracks. Only used for extended run films (roadshows).

As admission numbers continued to fall (nationally, admissions were 1396 million in 1950), something had to be done to arrest the decline and "Cinemascope" started being installed on Merseyside from 1954 onwards. Even this was not straightforward, as 20th Century Fox insisted that only cinemas with the full package could show their films. Rank refused on cost grounds, to equip all of their halls, but the newly established(on Merseyside) Essoldo circuit agreed and had a shot in the arm by showing Fox's output, to the chagrin of the Rank circuit hall managers. This did not preclude the others installing the system without stereo sound, it just meant that they could not get Fox films. As an outlet for their films, Fox leased the Futurist and the Scala in Lime Street, from 1954 until 1960. A lot of the older buildings should never have been converted. the prosceniums were far too narrow and whilst a new screen could sometimes be erected in front, constraints of the building, particularly where the screen was at the apex of a triangle, meant that little enlargement was possible. The end result was that the screen had to be masked down, lowering the top masking resulted in a 'letterbox' effect. In others the picture was little bigger than before! Hardly the 'panoramic wide screen' claimed and disappointing for patrons.

All the time, television was nibbling away at the audience figures. When Independant Television started in 1956, everything changed. This was not like the staid old BBC - and it had adverts! Apart from its own programmes, American import series were shown and even old films! When the government relaxed the law on bingo, (with the Betting and Gaming Act of 1960 allowing up-front cash betting) they thought that they were helping the vicar and his parishoners, play housey-housey in the church hall. Instead it allowed the creation of large bingo clubs and where better to house them, but in an old cinema! Alterations were minimal, as members were initially happy to sit in the existing cinema seats. Replace the screen with a numbers board, add a bar, some fruit machines and away you go! Many of the next decades closures were already sold for bingo, before they had closed. When Sidney Bernstein established Granada Television studios in Manchester, he is reputed to have said that it was because the area had the highest rainfall and therefore the most stay at home people! Who would want to leave the comfort of their fireside for a cold, draughty run down 'flea pit', which is what some of the 'palaces' had become. Couple that with the number of 'duff' films on release(and the circuits were contracted to take them!) and the inevitable result was closures.

There had always been cinemas closing for various reasons. At the beginning it was a move away from former billiard halls and churches to purpose built premises. Then the installation of sound cost too much for an independant to bear, so they 'took the money'. Lastly, cinemas were closed and demolished for the erection of larger and more modern ones or because of relocation. The Kings Hall in Oakfield Road, Anfield, closed in October 1930, was immediately demolished and the Gaumont Palace built. The Majestic in Daulby Street suffered a similar fate, closing in April 1937 and the Majestic 'super' opening in October of the same year. ABC had leased the Olympia, but it was too big and not in the city centre. When in 1931, they built the Forum in Lime Street they could relinquish the lease on the Liverpool Picture House, Clayton Square in 1936 and then closed the Olympia in 1939. This time it was rationalisation. Most Liverpudlians had a cinema within walking distance, but with the more run down halls unattractive to customers and losing money it was time to prune some deadwood. Going to the pictures had been a once or twice a week event, but now the 'box in the living room' was taking over. 1955 saw the opening of the Albany, Maghull, 1956 was when the new Bootle Gaumont rose from the ashes of the bombed out Broadway and the first wave of closures! Rank closed the Beresford, Dingle, Corona, Crosby and the Grand, Allerton. ABC abandoned the Coliseum, Walton, Coliseum, Paddington and the Popular on Netherfield Road North. These were all second run halls and 'tired'. During the rest of the decade, a steady trickle of closures continued. Whilst the independants bore the brunt of these, the circuits also continued paring away. Essoldo had its first cuts, closing the Atlas, Walton and the Garrick, Kirkdale. Bedford Cinemas(1928) Ltd also abandoned the oddly named Cabbage Hall in Anfield. The first of the 'supers' to go was the independant Ritz in Utting Avenue, after only 28 years. The first city centre closure was the Palais de Luxe in Lime Street in October 1959. Unable to install widescreen, yet competing with its neighbours who had, its fate was sealed.

Another factor began to come into play now, - vandalism. This was the 'Teddy Boy' era, where it was fun to slash cinema seats. At the Winter Gardens in Waterloo, it got so bad that the manager mounted seats in the foyer with a notice inviting patrons to slash these and not ours! The Reo in Fazakerley was the nearest cinema to the new housing estates at Kirkby, which resulted in an increasing amount of disruption to performances and damage. This drove the regular customers away, hastening closure. Films like "Rock Around the Clock" may have boosted takings, but at the price of dancing in the aisles, calling the police to restore order - and more damage!

Films of the decade, but not damage causing, included "The Titfield Thunderbolt"(1952) and other Ealing films. Disney's "Lady and the Tramp (1955), Cecil B. DeMille continued his 'epics' with "The Ten Commandments"(1956) and "Ben Hur"(1959) "Bridge on the River Kwai"(1957) plus a succession of Elvis and his pelvis!

Of the major circuits, Rank began to diversify in to other leisure areas, reducing its dependance on films. It was also involved with the regional Southern Television, whose Southampton studios were originally in a converted cinema! ABC adopted a ' if you can't beat them, join them' attitude by forming ABC TV Ltd and successfully bidding for ITV franchises.

THE1960's - BOND, BINGO AND BBC2

By 1960, countrywide admissions figures had slumped to 515 million, yet the decade started on a positive note with the abolition of Entertainment Tax in April 1960 and with ABC aquiring the Futurist in Lime Street, installing 70mm TODD-AO projectors and operating it as a 'roadshow' house. This was one film having an extended run. To do this at a normal cinema would have meant that patrons weekly visits would have been disrupted(they then may have just stayed in and watched the telly!) Musicals were popular, the first film shown was "Oklahoma" complete with six channel stereo sound. The Abbey in Wavertree in 1964 installed "Cinerama". This was three projectors in sync producing a giant picture on to a huge curved screen. A new projection room had to be built at the rear of the stalls and after re-seating, plus converting the upstairs lounge into Liverpools first cinema bar, some

£90,000 had been spent.

Outside of the city centre, the future was grim. Independants, circuit houses, supers, were all culled. By 1966 Essoldo had closed all of its suburban houses. By the end of the decade, Rank had only the Odeons(Plaza) in Crosby and Bootle(Gaumont). ABC, having been taken over by EMI in 1969, fared no better with just the former Astoria, Walton and the Carlton, Tuebrook. The only suburban independants left were the Woolton, Abbey and the Mayfair. Classic had bought the Allerton Odeon(Plaza) in 1967, re-naming it, but its future was under threat, due to the amount of land with it. One cinema that was still well attended was the Palladium on West Derby Road. An independant, it was a 'family house', catering especially for pensioners. When the scheme to make a dual carriageway was approved, it came under a Compulsory Purchase Order. Despite protests and a petition to 10 Downing Street, the order went through and it closed on July 1 1967, demolition commencing immediately.

In the city, no more closures occured, though the Scala, Lime Street, was operated by Gala Films from 1960 until 1968, as a 'continental' cinema with much 'X' rated material and good patronage. ABC then ran it, with a mixed film policy. The Tatler News Theatre in Church Street became a 'Classic' cinema in 1968 and then a cinema 'club' the following year. The other news theatre in Clayton Square, became a 'Gala' then a 'Jacey', with 'X' rated films.The Odeon on London Road was divided into two screens in 1968. Televisions continued to improve, with bigger and better screens, plus technical refinements. The BBC started a second channel, using the superior 625 line system and did colour test transmissions in 1966. The author can remember seeing a crowd round a shop in Bold Street, watching a TV showing a picture in colour!

An emerging problem was what to do with the growing numbers of redundant cinemas. Being built for one specific purpose, options were limited, but two new uses were found. Ten Pin Bowling had arrived from America and ABC started converting stadium type cinemas into bowling alleys. The ABC Regal, Litherland closed in July 1962 and work to convert it started immediately, opening for bowling in January, the following year. Another alley was built next to the ABC Carlton in Tuebrook. The craze was short lived and they both ended up eventually as nightclubs. After the Capitol in Overton Street, Edge Hill closed it was initially a warehouse for Freemans, but then it it was demolished for a new store and bowling alley. The other new use was more lasting - bingo. When the Garrick closed it was vandalised, but was resurrected as a bingo club in the early 1960's, such was the demand! One advantage was that there was money for improvements/repairs that the cinema owners never had. Interior decorations were preserved and sometimes restored. The downside was that additional direct lighting and 'bingo colours' destroyed the effect that the designers intended. In later years, floors were levelled to install flat table bingo, false ceilings hid the originals and acres of plasterboard obscured the elaborate mouldings. Now, purpose built clubs have replaced most of those that had survived. Bingo is still alive, but the golden age of it is over.

One or two buildings found a new purpose as supermarkets, or car showrooms, but some were just left to rot! Initially, upon closure, all cinema related items would be recovered, leaving little more than a shell. But as the closure rate accelerated, a lot of stuff was deemed just not worth recovering.

Once thieves and vandals had gained access, the structures rapidly deteriorated until enforced demolition was the only option. Apart from smashing every single pane of glass, one of the favourite vandals tricks was to get into the roof void and kick holes in the ceiling. Having once stood in the wrecked auditorium of the Walton Vale Picture House in 1961, it was a depressing experience. Everything that could be smashed, had been and a lot of the ceiling was full of kick holes. the screen had been ripped into slivers and the once proud festoon curtain was also ripped and hung drunkenly. There was a layer of debris underfoot and a smell that only a decaying building can produce. I can only think that the wreckers ball provided a merciful release! Both the Popular in Everton and the Atlas in Walton were just left for decades, the former closing in 1956, not being demolished until the 1970's whilst the latter closed in 1958 and lasted until 1981!
Offerings for the filmgoers that were left included James Bonds adventures, the Beatles and Cliff Richards singing their way through the decade, plus the advent of the 'spaghetti western'. The 'Carry On' British sex comedies continued to deplete the supply of innuendos, while Disney kept animation alive with "101 Dalmations"(1961) amongst others. "Doctor Zhivago"(1965), "The Graduate"(1967), "Easy Rider"(1969) and "Butch Cassidy and the Sundance Kid"(1969), were top earners and who could forget "Mary Poppins"(1964)?

THE 1970'S - END OF AN ERA

Total cinema admissions bottomed in 1970 at 193 million. Colour television was on all three channels and during the decade, domestic video recorders made their debut. Now you could record films, or rent them from the mushrooming hire shops, to view at your convenience at home. There was no longer enough patrons to make the larger halls profitable, but the owners found the solution in sub-division. The idea was that different programmes would attract a wider audience, making the screens profitable. Economies in labour could be achieved by combining projection rooms and letting people find their own seats. One paybox would suffice. Advances in automation meant that operator numbers could be slashed. Other income could be generated by maximising kiosk sales. The Odeon had already been 'twinned' in 1968, allowing a roadshow in one, while weekly changing programmes continued in the other. At the ABC (Carlton), Tuebrook, 1972 saw the rear stalls converted, by a drop wall, into a separate western themed bar called "The Painted Wagon" (reminds you of a film?) The company created others with the same name elswhere. The Classic (Odeon), Crosby was 'tripled' in 1976. In Maghull, the Albany became the Astra Entertainment Centre, with 4 screens, in 1975. Back in town, the Odeon 2 was further sub-divided into 3 in 1973 and the bar became yet another screen in 1979, just plain 'boxes' with a screen! The downside to conversions was that the original decorations were usually lost, either destroyed or hidden behind the ubiquitous plasterboard! The closures still continued, with the enormous Hippodrome at the top of West Derby Road in May 1970. The Majestic, Daulby Street, followed a month later. One of the last independants, the site was required for the new Royal Hospital and immediate demolition followed. In April 1971, the Allerton Classic closed its doors, but the redevelopment that followed incorporated a smaller cinema, which opened in 1973 as the Classic! The same company shut their Church Street one earlier (March) that year. Conversion to a church was the fate of the Jacey in Clayton Square after July 1972. On Aigburth Road, the Mayfair bowed out in June 1973, showing (appropiately) "The Last Picture Show". Walton lost the ABC (Astoria) in February 1974 and May was the end for the Gaumont, Camden Street, made redundant by the conversion of the Odeon. After only 19 years, the Bootle Odeon succumbed in November 1975. The last casualty of the decade, in August 1979, was the mighty Abbey in Wavertree. The problem with it was that, apart from it's size, there were not enough Cinerama films made to keep it showing them all the time, therefore it lost its unique advantage.

There was, however, one opening, in 1975. At the junction of Brownlow Hill and Mount Pleasant, ironically on the site of the one time New Century Picture Hall, the Star group built an entertainments complex including a three screen cinema, with 215, 130 and 140 seats respectively. They were extremely basic, consisting of a screen with masking, no curtains or stage and a plain-walled auditorium(described as 'modern, clean, lines', by the press). Named "Studio 1, 2 and 3", the intention was to offer a contrasting range of films, but were denied a supply of first runs because ABC and Rank had cinemas nearby. Instead, there was a gradual drift towards 'X' certificate programmes, until that was all that they showed. Despite different operators, types of films and name changes to the Ritz and then the 051, nothing seemed to make it pay and it closed in September 1997.

This was the special effects decade with "the Towering Inferno"(1975), which was shown at the Futurist after installation of a 'Sensurround' sound sysytem. This was so realistic that it caused cracks in the wall plaster! "Jaws" arrived in the same year but two years later, Sci-Fi took off big time with "Star Wars" and "Close Encounters of the Third Kind". "Grease" kept the musical alive, but not like a Rogers and Hammerstein production! Never one to be outwitted, Mr. Bond just kept on pulling the girls.

THE 1980'S TO DATE - IT'S CINEMA, BUT NOT AS WE KNEW IT

The first major change occurred in May 1982, when the ABC (Forum) in Lime Street closed for conversion to a triple. With over 1800 seats, this was the last of the large single screen Liverpool cinemas and had become almost impossible to fill anymore. A narrow proscenium width had made it a less than ideal candidate for Cinemascope, the picture having to be masked down to about twelve feet. its competition, the Odeons, had no such constraints. The £350.000 project involved creating two screens in the former stalls (272 and 217 seats), with a new combined projection room at the rear. The balcony was retained, with a new wide screen erected in front of the proscenium. Another new projection room was built at the rear, equipped for 70 or 35mm film and Dolby stereo sound. Seating capacity was 683, down from the original 750. Re-opening in August, this then meant the end for the Futurist and Scala, across the road. There was now sufficient capacity in the Forum for three different programmes, previously that would have needed three separate cinemas! The Futurist duly closed in July, the Scala following the following month. Due to restrictive covernants attached to their sale, buyers for the two buildings were difficult to find. The Scala eventually became the "Hippodrome" club in 1987 and ended up as a nightclub, to date. The Futurist remains empty and in a terrible condition inside. The last suburban ABC in Tuebrook(Carlton) closed its doors in November 1982, but for its final two years had been leased out, reverting to its original name. That left only the Plaza, Crosby (a Cannon from 1986), the Allerton Odeon and the Woolton in suburbia, with the Odeon, Studio's and Forum(also now a Cannon) servicing the city centre.

But then the cinema began to strike back! Computerised special effects were progressively developed and a steady stream of 'blockbusters' kept the public interest. The creation of smaller multiple screens by division had proved profitable, so the next logical step was to purpose build complexes of several screens or Multiplexes. The first local one was Showcase Cinemas and was on the East Lancashire Road at Gillmoss, opening in December 1989. This was eye catching and had a large car park (important now in a car society). Having 12 screens, you could always watch something and the foyer was laid out to maximise kiosk sales (unlike decades ago, when a cashier told her manager how much the confectionery sales were up, only to get the retort that " we are here to sell films, not sweets! ") The auditoriums may have been basic 'boxes', with no atmosphere, but the public took to the concept. With comfortable seating, plenty of leg room and good heating and ventilating, they were a far cry from the 'flea pits' of old. The abolition of smoking also added to the appeal, as there was no longer the danger of ending up smelling like an ashtray! Disabled access was incorporated to all the screens, which were on one floor. Only one projector was required per screen, as the whole film programme was wound on a horizontal 'cakestand', from which it was taken out of the centre, passed through the projector and returned to the outside of the reel. No rewinding was required and with a high power bulb replacing the arc, full automation meant the whole show could be started remotely. The latest in stereo sound systems were also incorporated. If two adjacent screens showed the same film, it could be looped through the second projector as well and shown again a few seconds later in the next screen.

The next multiplex to open was the 8 screen MGM in the Edge Lane Retail Park, in August 1991. this had further technical improvements including a computerised booking system. The location was no accident as you could now do your shopping and go to the pictures, all in one place. Odeon opened another 12 screen one at Switch Island, between Aintree and Maghull.

The Albany/Astra in Northway, Maghull, finally closed in April, 1995. It had been converted into two mini-cinemas and a bingo hall in 1975 and then four screens in 1981, after bingo patronage declined. Planning permission was granted for a supermarket in 1998, the building was demolished and a Lidl now occupies the site.

On the 29 January 1998, the former Forum, Lime Street, bowed out in style. after progressively losing custom to the multiplexes and the five screen Odeon, which had first runs of the most successful films.

The final film was "Casablanca", which had its first run here in 1943. There was a queue all the way down Lime Street, just like the old days! Because of its listed building status, the options for re-use are limited and to date it is unused, although the stonework has been restored. Most of the art-deco interior is also still intact.

The first decade of the new millennium saw the saving of the Plaza in Crosby. Since 1995, when the owners, the Apollo group, had announced plans to sell it for demolition and redevelopment, a concerted campaign had been organised to keep it open. Leasing it of a development company initially, with an option to purchase. Three days before this ran out, enough funds had been raised to purchase it and the option was exercised, becoming the property of the Crosby Community Cinema in January 2000. There was the demolition of the former Bedford, Walton in 2007. This was the first purpose built cinema in Liverpool and was the subject of an unsuccessful campaign to list it. All the decorative stonework had been smashed off the facade, to forestall any preservation attempts. The Woolton was sold by Cheshire County Cinemas in1992 to David Wood, whose grandfather built the Bedford and together with his father, ran the Bedford Cinemas (1928) Ltd circuit. When David sadly died in 2006 it closed down in that September. The building was put up for sale and bought by a consortium, who then re-opened it in March 2007. 2008 saw the Odeon in London Road closed and a purpose built 14 screen multiplex opened in October, as part of the Liverpool 1 shopping development. The other Odeon in Allerton Road, gave its last performance in February, 2009.

Whilst the number of screens across the country has continued to increase, that is not true of the number of cinemas. The days of large single screen houses have gone, being replaced by multiple screens, in whatever format. That there are still people who appreciate seeing a film in a cinema, rather than on a television, is heartening in this DVD age. How we arrived at this stage, is what this book is about and is worthy of keeping from obscurity. The buildings that are left contain many reminders of their past, of a socially important part of our history that is now consigned to fading memories.

CASE STUDY - THE RICE LANE PICTURE HOUSE (ATLAS)

This was constructed on a triangular site with Rice Lane on the west side and a wide passage called Throstles Nest, leading to the Northcote Road streets on the east. It was opened on the 16 May 1914 and had an original capacity of 1,000, including a balcony seating about 300. The auditorium had a curved ceiling with a wreath of leaves design round the circular extract grilles and the side walls had a panel effect by using raised plaster mouldings. Main lighting was by large, single bulbs within glass shades, which were suspended from the ceiling. Three cleaners lights were also provided, consisting of bare 250 watt bulbs, one above the front and rear stalls, plus over the balcony. Secondary lighting consisted of single mantle, swan neck gas fittings with glass shades. These were located at intervals along the auditorium walls, above the electrically lit exit signs, stairs landings and public areas. The ones in the auditorium had red shades. The screen was at the apex end, but the auditorium only splayed out slightly before the side walls became parallel all the way to the rear. The space thus created was used for toilets and emergency exits on the eastern side. The Rice Lane side housed the main entrance, with a ticket window. A wide passage extended across the rear of the building, for queueing patrons, This had a handrail down the centre and a large mirror at the far end. To the right of the entrance, a wide return marble staircase led to a lounge area, off which was the managers office, a store and a room containing the incoming electrical supply, distribution equipment and the motor generator sets.

There was also a large panel of light switches for the inside, outside and cleaners lights. From the lounge, access could be gained to the balcony front. The rear was reached by a continuation of the main staircase, which terminated in a small lobby. Straight ahead, double doors opened onto the rear balcony crossover passage and a door marked 'private' on the eastern side led to the projection suite. This was up a flight of stone steps and consisted of a rewind, non-sync and projection rooms. In the latter, a hand windlass on the auditorium dividing wall operated the screen curtains. At the head of the stairs, past the first steel firedoor, was a door that led out onto a small area of flat roof, with a water tank in one corner. On the Rice Lane side of the auditorium, at stalls level, doors led to toilets and the boiler room. Set into the pavement outside was a steel trap door, through which coke was delivered into a cellar. Next to it was a room containing a large coke-fired boiler, which powered the radiators that heated the building. The hot water circulation was primarily by gravity, but to the side of the boiler was a hand operated pump(with a long handle that would not be out of place in a farmyard!) to increase the flow, when more heating was needed. Rising out of the roadside cellar wall was a large lead pipe with a stopcock, which was the mains water supply and something else to catch yourself on!

The proscenium arch was almost at the apex of the building, there only being a set of store rooms behind, with the windows looking down Rice Lane. The restricted space meant that the screen was quite small and set higher than usual above the stage. The maximum picture size would be about 16 feet wide by 12 feet high. From the road, the front stalls access was via a small foyer and paybox at the 'sharp end'.

Outside, the main road elevation was of brick, relieved by bands of white terra-cotta. Above the parapet at the top of the wall the were three features at evenly spaced intervals. These consisted of a panel with a wreath of leaves, also in white. A canopy ran the whole length of the building, useful for queuing for the trams/buses that stopped outside. Throstles Nest, in contrast, was treated to a plain brick wall, relieved only by a fine display of cast iron and lead wastepipes! The name "Atlas" was displayed in large, vertical, neon-lit letters on the apex wall after re-naming in 1932.

When it opened, it was described as 'luxurious' with its marble floors, comfortable seating and potted plants. Originally, competition was only the Bedford, by Walton Church and possibly the Queens, on Walton Road. In 1922, the Walton Vale Picture House opened, only a short tram ride away. Finally the Carlton in Moss Lane, Orrell Park, arrived on the scene. A month after this, the first sound film, "Hearts in Exile" was shown. The original screen was painted on the wall, so to allow for a chamber to house the speaker horns, a new perforated one was erected in front. The cinema was closed for re-seating and redecoration in the Egyptian style in 1932. Spacing out the seats more, reduced the seating capacity to 800. Seats in the front or pit stalls were hard wooden tip-up ones, the balcony and rear stalls had tip-ups that were upholstered and finished in green plush. Curtains covering the screen were also green, to match.

Films shown were always later runs of the big circuits releases, plus some off circuit ones. This was the main reason that it was not popular. Nearby,

THE RICE LANE PICTURE HOUSE

Two external views, top shows after closure in 1958, above is the frontage to Rice Lane in 1973.

THE RICE LANE PICTURE HOUSE

Interior in 1981, just prior to demolition. The original screen was painted on the wall, but a sound chamber was needed for the 'talkies', resulting in a perforated screen in front. The framing is still there on the left. Below is the pit stalls entrance from Rice Lane.

This is the rear stalls, looking towards Rice Lane, .fragments of the plasterwork are still visible. The left hand door was the entrance from the foyer, whilst the right hand one was to toilets and emergency exit.

the locals could see the just released films, instead of having to wait for them to be shown here, after everybody else had seen them! When opened in 1914, it was part of the G. Gordon's circuit, in 1932 The Rice Lane Picture House Company, 1938 Southan Morris circuit and finally Essoldo inherited it in 1954. Surprisingly there was never any change to what was a less than ideal booking policy.

After the 1932 'modernisation' no further works were carried out, as a result it became more and more rundown. By the time that Essoldo aquired it as part of the Southan Morris sale it had become one of the notorious 'flea pits'. One child that managed to 'bunk' into a performance, said years later that he had "itched for hours afterwards"! The fact that it was impossible to install a wider screen, coupled with generally falling admissions meant that it was one of the first of Essoldo's Liverpool closures on 1 March 1958. An idea of how bad the state of it was can be deduced from the fact that only the projectors and sound equipment were recovered. The motor generators, seats, screen, curtains and everything else was just abandoned. This was the period when a closed cinema would normally be stripped bare!

The building became increasingly derelict and vandalised and although it sported a sign stating that it had been aquired by the Wirral firm of 'Telegraph Garages Ltd', nothing happened. The canopy, sign and the decorative roof parapet panels became dangerous and were removed, followed by the roof slates later in the 1970's. Demolition finally took place in November 1981, with the surrounding properties following a few years later. The Northcote Road area has now been redeveloped with new housing, a supermarket and a filling station. The Walton Citadel of the Salvation Army, which was next to the Queens cinema in Walton road, has also relocated to here.

This is a very typical example of an early suburban cinema in a working class district. It is also proof that being situated in a heavily populated area does not automatically guarantee a lot of customers. When it was built there was nothing fancy about it. The 1932 upgrading might have made it slightly more appealing at the time but the main problem all its life was the film bookings. It was disadvantaged more when the modern supers opened, offering first runs and far greater comfort. having a Gaumont(Bedford) and 3 ABC's (Astoria,Victory and Reo) reasonably near barred it from taking their circuit releases. The main road through the area also made it easy to travel to a better cinema with newly released films. The downward spiral of diminishing returns then kicked in, meaning that no money was spent upgrading the building. When it closed, it still had the original sanitary ware and plumbing, an inefficient heating system and had not been decorated for many years, it was indeed worthy of the 'flea pit' title! Liverpool had quite a few halls like this in poorer districts and like this one, were early casualties because they had become unattractive to patronise. Television cannot be wholly blamed for their demise as they really caused it themselves.

CASE STUDY - THE CLOSING NIGHT AT THE FORUM

This was an imposing cinemas on a prime site in Lime Street. It was built by ABC and opened in 1931. It was the last single screen cinema in the city to be converted, becoming a triple in 1982. The final period of operation was as a 'Cannon', the group having aquired the remaining ABC cinemas from EMI in 1987. Increasing losses led to a closure date of Thursday, January 29 1998.

Almost all cinema closures happened without marking the(sad) occasion, patrons watching the last programme, filing out and then the lights going out for ever. This was not going to happen at the Forum.

The manageress, Julie Pilkington, decided that it should bow out 'in a blaze of glory'. Suitable press releases resulted in extensive coverage by the local papers and even on television. For the final week, the canopy display board advertised "The Last picture show on Lime Street". It was decided that the final film would be "Gone With the Wind", but it was unavailable so the projectionist Derek Minshull's choice of "Casablanca" was obtained instead. Derek, himself had started his career at the Curzon on Prescot road and when that closed in August 1960, got himself a job 'across the road', at the ABC Regent. The following year he was summoned to see his manager, who informed him that he was being transferred to the Forum, at which he stayed, notching up 37 years! He loved the building and could remember its heyday, when it had an organ and impressive cove lighting, now he had the saddest job of all, closing it down.

Advance tickets cost the same as when the film had its Liverpool premiere here in 1943, 10p (two shillings).

The day arrived and a scene from decades ago unfolded on Lime Street, - a huge queue all the way back to beyond where the Palais de Luxe used to be! Sheer weight of numbers overwhelmed the staff, once the doors were opened, in fact the start of the show had to be delayed until everybody was inside and seated. The music was Dereks own records, specially chosen to represent the period of the film. Then the lights went down and the full house clapped in anticipation. first on the screen was a reel of vintage trailers, lent by one of Dereks fellow projectionists. The audience were once again exhorted to see "Gone With The Wind", "The Glen Miller Story" and "Seven Brides For Seven Brothers". A selection of the old confectionery adverts followed, the final one with the ABC cartoon dance band saying to get your ice cream from the sales girls NOW! Then the girls appeared for real complete with the ice cream! Yes, it was for sale, just like years ago.

The manageress, Julie, then went on stage with a male staff member at each side. The men wore immaculate evening suits, while a black thirties style evening dress complete with gloves befitted the lady.

Through a microphone, she thanked every body for coming to the last show. One former wartime ex- employee was called up to receive a bouquet of flowers. Then Derek was asked to come down from the box to receive an award. Amidst deafening applause, he descended the long flight of stairs, somewhat reluctantly gained the stage and was thanked for his long devotion to the most vital part of the cinema. Overcome with emotion, he kissed Julie and returned to his box, accompanied by more enthusiastic clapping.

There then followed a lengthy pause, no doubt while a tearful Derek composed himself and the the house lights went down, the curtain rose for the last time and "Casablanca" was shown again. At the end, the audience left in silence, No music was played as Derek said that there was nothing suitable to end such an era. His career ended that night, as he retired along with the Forum!

This begs the question that if so many people were prepared to turn out for this 'wake', then why could not at least some of them patronise the ordinary shows and thus help to keep it in business? Part of the Forum's problem lies in its location. When it was built it was one of the 'supers', with a luxurious art-

THE END OF THE FORUM

29 January 1998, the queue is like the old days

The last day, Derek Minshull in front of the Forum.
The interval with the manageress and staff on stage.
Derek was called down to take a bow for his loyal service
The whole evening was a celebration rather than a funeral.

deco interior complete with organ. With few people owning cars, it was in an ideal position to be supplied with patrons using public transport from each side of the city. Showing first run ABC circuit films it did attract a lot of clientele, for this was the only place to see the new circuit releases. The decline in post war cinemagoers has already been explained, but the fact that the installation of widescreen was compromised by the proscenium width must have diverted some potential customers to the Odeon, which had no such problems. When it was tripled in 1982, the widescreen issue was resolved by erecting a new screen forward of the original proscenium, now ABC1, but two more factors now came into play. One was that the 5 screen Odeon was getting the better films, the other was the growth of the suburban multiplexes, which were more local and had free car parking, not to mention a lot greater choice of films. this is what left the Forum out on a limb - market forces. Unlike the Atlas, the building was modernised, clean and well maintained, but that is not the whole recipe for success.

Because it is a Grade 2 Listed Building, options for re-use are limited. To date it lies empty but intact, though in 2008 the foyer and canopy lights were lit again when it was used as an information centre, in connection with the "Capital of Culture" but the entrances to the screens were blocked off with sheets of plywood.

CASE STUDY - THE DERBY PICTUREDROME, SCOTLAND ROAD

At the corner of Scotland Road and Wilbraham Street, the Scotland Road United Methodist Church was built in 1843, with seats for 400. In 1852 it broke away as a Wesleyan Reform Church, but returned to the fold in the following year. The next decade saw a great wave of revivalist activity and in 1866 the church was enlarged to seat 700, including adding a gallery. The district became increasingly populated by Roman Catholics, which led to a dwindling congregation to the point where it was uneconomic. Accordingly the Trustees put the building up for sale in 1910, with an asking price of £2000, but the best offer was £565, from a Mr. E. Haigh, an early cinema circuit operator. The Trustees were minded to place a restrictive covernant, forbidding any form of entertainment, on the building, but were advised that it would be rendered unsaleable, by their solicitor. Still losing money, the sale was agreed at a meeting on the 20 June 1911, the church was closed and the furnishings distributed to other churches in the Methodist circuit.

Mr Haigh wasted no time, adding a new facade, to include the foyer and projection suite. External covered stairways were built on each side, to get to the balcony and a passage added on the Wilbraham Street side accessing the front stalls. The Cinematograph Licence was granted on the 14 October 1912.

The auditorium formed was long and narrow, with the balcony extending over half of it. Seating capacity was originally 1,100. In 1929, with the 'talkies' on the way, an extension at the rear was constructed. This was wider than the original structure and had a curved ceiling, unlike the existing flat church type one.

The seating capacity was increased to 1,240 and it was now even longer! Films shown were later runs of the major circuit releases, but despite similar halls competing in the area, the attraction of low prices and being in a very densely populated district ensured its survival. Unsuitable for Cinemascope,

THE DERBY PICTUREDROME SCOTLAND ROAD
These are the interior views, to illustrate the case study

The proscenium, with the sound chamber at the rear. The vertical rods are the false ceiling hanger and the pipe was feeding the central heating, put in by Whitneys.

Right middle, The frontage of the building in 2009. Above the sheeting is the church gable end.

The 1866 church ceiling

Above, The 1929 extension ceiling
Right, 1929 side wall, showing the basic plasterwork and the former windows that every cinema had to have. The height of the false ceiling is indicated by where the orange stops!

closure came on the 14 May 1960, along with Byrom Picture Houses other cinema, the Gaiety, further along the road. Slum clearances were under way, reducing the population, plus the allure of the 'telly'!

Across the road, George Vickers had a used car sales pitch, trading under the name of Whitneys. They purchased the building and altered it in 1961 into a car showroom. This involved the removal of the outside and inside stairways, sealing up the 1911 extension above ground floor level and the removal of the balcony. A false ceiling was installed, together with a resited central heating system, powered by a new oil boiler in the basement. At the screen end was created a repair garage, with a new door punched through the wall onto Wilbraham Street. On the frontage, a fine display of neon advertised what it was now. At the end of the decade, the facade was covered in steel sheeting, to go with the 'modern' age, so hiding any indications of its past, except for the gable end of the main roof.

The next owner of the building by 1982 was a firm of funeral directors, who erected a labyrinth of stud walls to form offices and chapels of rest. The rear end was used for hearses and embalming was also carried out on the premises. This business was transferred in 2007 to the former Grosvenor cinema on Stanley Road, which the company had aquired in 1995. Sold with planning for a block of flats, it slumbers awaiting the bulldozers, but the front part was used as a firework shop in autumn 2009. The rest of the inside is partially gutted, revealing the layers of alterations.

This is an example of how complicated the history of a building can be and thousands must pass it, without a thought, every day.

CASE STUDY - THE DINGLE PICTUREDROME / GAUMONT, PARK ROAD

The Dingle Picturedrome was the first purpose-built cinema in south Liverpool. All the other existing cinemas in the area had been conversions of existing buildings. The architects, Campbell and Fairhurst designed it and with 770 seats, opened in December 1912 after the licence was granted on the 6th of the month. It was built for T. H. Hughes and E Haigh(one of the early pioneers), who formed the Dingle Picturedrome Ltd as an operating company(this was common practice, having a separate company for each cinema, so that the failure of one would not bring down the others, despite having the same directors). Thomas Halliwell Hughes also had built, the Grand, Empress and Beresford, giving him a circuit of four cinemas.

As early as 1919, plans were put forward for a larger, replacement building, along with a new cinema on the corner of Beresford Road/Park Road. The latter was built, named the Beresford and with a seating capacity of 1047, had a licence granted on 26 January 1922. Nothing further was done, as regards the Dingle. The nearest cinema was the Aigburth Picture House, converted from a public hall and this also came under the control of the Halliwell Hughes circuit after 1920. With the public having an insatiable appetite for moving pictures, the halls were profitable, comfortable or not!

In March 1928, the circuit was sold to Denman Picture Houses, which then became part of Gaumont British. As the valuation of the Dingle was only £4,800 and they had aquired cinemas on each side of it, the cost of converting it for sound was not considered to be worthwhile and it was closed in 1930. John F. Wood had also sold his Bedford Cinemas circuit to Denman in 1928, but then set up a new company, Bedford Cinemas (1928) Ltd and

announced plans to build a super cinema in Aigburth Road by Lark Lane. It has been said that this is what precipitated the building of the Gaumont.
In 1935, the Dingle was demolished, along with the premises of the South End Motor Company, which were on the corner of Dingle Lane. Part of the corner was used for road improvements, leaving a fan shaped site. Gaumont's architect, W. E. Trent, exploited this by producing a curved facade, relieved by bands of different coloured bricks and a splayed auditorium. Above the curved balcony was a rectangular recess, at the back of which were the projection ports. this, or a dome, were a feature of the new-build Gaumonts, but resulted in a steep projection rake, to which the screen had to be set back to compensate. The internal passages also mirrored the curve. Opening on 29 March 1937, it seated 885 in the stalls and 615 in the balcony. A WurliTzer organ was also installed with art-deco grilles each side of the screen for the pipe chambers. This was removed from the Trocadero in Camden Street. A month later, formidable competition arrived, with the opening of John F. Wood's Mayfair on Aigburth Road. This mostly played the first suburban ABC releases, whist the Gaumont ran its own equivalent. When attendances declined in the 1950's, Rank, who were now in control, first closed the older, smaller halls each side. The Beresford finished on 29 September 1956 and the Aigburth Picture House, now called the Rivoli, followed on 5 January 1957. Even so, it became increasingly difficult to attract enough patrons to be profitable. The circuit release was not always popular (but they had to take it!) and there was always the ever improving telly as competition! A dispute between Rank and 20th Century Fox over Cinemascope installation(which barred them from showing Fox Cinemascope) did not help, but the final film, "Those Magnificent Men in Their Flying Machines" rolled on 17 September 1966. Conversion to bingo quickly followed, re-opening as a Top Rank Bingo Club on 13 October. Redecorated in 'bingo colours' it flourished in the boom years that followed, but falling attendances and the rising costs of maintaining and heating such a large building, caused a move to a former modern supermarket, further up Park Road. Closure was on 2 April 1997, with the new club opening the following day.
Following stripping out, the building was put up for sale and it was eventually sold to a couple who wanted to develop it as a multi-purpose venue and community centre. Despite Rank having a liquor licence, a new application was refused. A lot of work was carried out on the building, only for youngsters to break in and cause extensive vandalism, including trying to set it on fire! Unable to raise the money to complete the restoration and with the bank calling in their loan, the proporty was repossessed. It was advertised for sale at £500,000, freehold, in winter 2009, but with the lack of car parking and nearby residents an issue, it is difficult to see what use the building can now be put to. Luckily, the organ was removed for preservation before the end of bingo.
This case study is a good example of how the cinema industry developed and the reasons for building one.

THE GAUMONT, PARK ROAD ,DINGLE

The vandalised interior, still in bingo colours, in 2009. The projection ports were in the ceiling.

GALLERY

How many of these do you know about?

THE ABBEY CINEMA HIGH STREET WAVERTREE

Perhaps Liverpools ultimate super, seating 1876 when opened in March 1939. Part of Bedford Cinemas(1928) from 1943.

Cinerama was installed in March 1964 with a giant screen. A new projection room was built in the rear stalls, but too few of the films negated the appeal.

ABBEY CINERAMA
(Near Site of Liverpool Show)
RUN EXTENDED TO NOV. 19.
ON THE GIANT SCREEN
WEST SIDE STORY (A)
Evgs. 7.30. Weds. & Sats. 2.30.
5/-, 7/6, 10/-. All bookable.
NOV. 20: OLIVIER In OTHELLO
CAR PARK. LICENSED BAR.

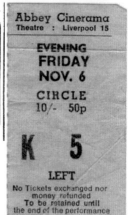

Abbey Cinerama
Theatre : Liverpool 15
EVENING
FRIDAY
NOV. 6
CIRCLE
10/- 50p
K 5
LEFT
No Tickets exchanged nor money refunded
To be retained until the end of the performance

Closed in August, 1979, it is now a supermarket with a snooker hall above.

1971 ticket

New projection room with 3 machines to make up the composite image. The throws had to be horizontal. To avoid distortion.

THE ALBANY NORTHWAY MAGHULL

The first post-war built cinema, seating 1400 and opening in September 1955. Renamed Astra and converted to a twin, plus bingo in 1975.

The bingo became 2 further screens in 1981. Finally closing in April 1995, a supermarket allowed in 1998

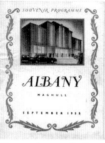

Opening night

THE BERESFORD PARK ROAD DINGLE

Built in 1922, it was part of the Gaumont circuit from 1928. From 1937 competing with the super just down the road, its 1047 seats made this tired hall one of the first wave of 1956 closures.

After its bingo reprieve which ended when the Gaumont did the same in 1966, demolition is awaited in April 1967

CLASSIC/CANNON/ODEON ALLERTON ROAD ALLERTON

A 493 seat stadium type on the first floor of the redevelopment of the Plaza site. Opening August 1973, it survived until February 2009.

In no frills 'multiplex' style. Food is as important as films...if not more!

In the auditorium, side curtains covered plain brickwork. We are seeing the transition to a 'basic' multiplex format.

The projection room had one projector, the entire programme being taken from the middle of the 'cakestand' on the left hand side, returning to the outside of it. No rewinds!

Fully automated, just press and go! The arc is now an Xenon bulb, so no more juggling with carbon rods!

THE ASTORIA WALTON ROAD KIRKDALE

A 1949 exterior

Opened in July 1930 by Astoria Entertainments, owners of the nearby Victory. Under ABC from 1935, it had 1586 seats and a proscenium width of 31 feet. Lasting until February 1974, as an ABC, it was vandalised but became a club in 1984. By the 90's it was bingo but when that was transferred to Paradise Island it was sold, demolished 2005. The large balcony is how you had such a capacity

Both pictures from 1951 show the "Mexican Aztec" style of decoration by the architects, Gray & Evans. Also, a flyer for the Astoria Club.

The Astoria Walton Road Kirkdale continued

Bingo in 1997, with a false ceiling. The last picture show as it is reduced to rubble in 2005.
When the cinemas were re-branded as ABC's, the former names were hidden. The Astoria Club removed the board re-instating its name.

THE BEDFORD HALL BEDFORD ROAD WALTON

This was the first purpose built cinema in Liverpool. Built by John F. Wood, founder of the Bedford circuit, it seated 1250, reduced to 835 with proper seats. The circuit was bought by Gaumont in 1928. New waiting room/entrance added in 1930's.

Closing in 1959, it became an auction room and finally a furniture shop. Listing was refused and it was demolished 2007.

A fairy tale? 1995
Ornate waiting area and entrance in 2006.

Above; after demolition
Left; ceiling decorations and projection ports in 2006. Balcony Rear height is current floor level.

THE BIJOU ELECTRIC PALACE EAST ST. WATERLOO
Built 1840 as a Methodist chapel, it became a 300 seat theatre with pictures
and variety in 1909, then a cinema from 1917.

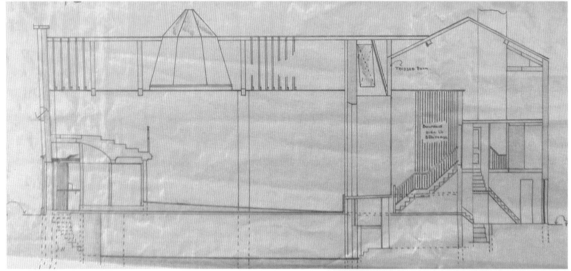

The letter and plan refer to work required by the magistrates to comply with the 1921 Act., to further improve safety. The estimates must have been too much as it closed in 1922. The main alteration was to move the box to the rear of the balcony. Later a garage, demolished 1990's for flats

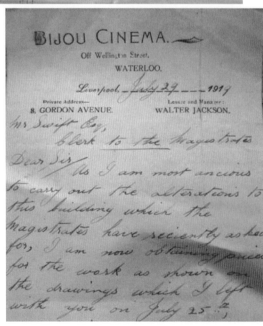

THE BROADWAY, STANLEY ROAD, BOOTLE

Opened in 1912, this was typical of the early purpose built halls. Destroyed in an air raid, May 1941, site later used for the Gaumont, though not until 1956.

Note the very small screen due to limitations of projector lamp and low ceiling.

THE BROADWAY continued

The rear auditorium. It could get foggy with the smokers!

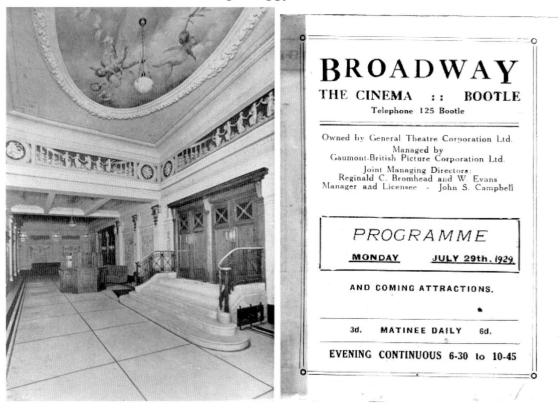

Quite an imposing entrance hall.

Programme from 1929

THE CABBAGE HALL PICTURE HOUSE LOWER BRECK ROAD

Another City Cinema Shuts
Cabbage Hall For Sale

The Cabbage Hall Picture House, Lower Breck Road, Liverpool, has been closed and is for sale.

Opened in 1913, the cinema seats 586, and is owned by Bedford Cinemas (1928) Ltd., of 19 Castle Street Liverpool.

Last July the company closed their Stella Cinema at Seaforth.

LOCAL PATRONAGE

These two cinemas were of the smaller type particularly dependent upon the patronage of local families, and therefore particularly vulnerable to television competition a company spokesman told the *Echo* to-day.

"We are not thinking of closing any of our other cinemas," he added.

Thirty-six cinemas have now closed down on Merseyside since December, 1956.

The most recent closure was that of the Garrick Picture House, Westminster Road, Bootle, which closed last month.

On April 22, three Rank cinemas will be offered for sale by auction. They are the Magnet, Picton Road, Wavertree; the Empress, Tuebrook; and the Bedford, Bedford Road, Walton.

A most odd Brassica related name! This was a 600 seater stadium type, opening in November 1913. Owned by Bedford Cinemas(1928) Ltd from 1943, showing later releases, it lasted until 31 January 1959.

Right, 1915 war time view.

Left, April 1959 Cutting from Echo

Below, As Liverpool Supporters Club in the early 1960's, plus a Ford Anglia. Bottom left, 1965 shot with vintage concrete bus shelter! After a 1972 fire, the front was rebuilt.

Above, as is today
Left, rebuilding in 1972 after the fire

THE CAMEO WEBSTER ROAD WAVERTREE

A church converted to a 690 seater stadium type, opening in October 1926. On Saturday 19 March 1949, a gunman shot the manager and his assistant, escaping with the days takings of about £50.00.

Gaumont controlled from 1928, the showing of later runs meant that it was an early casualty, closing in January 1957. Still sporting its name in 1958, later use included a kitchen firm, before demolition

THE CASINO PRESCOT ROAD KENSINGTON

August 1923 saw the opening of this large 1659 seater. Gaumont aquired it in 1928 and Cinemascope was no problem with a 60 foot wide proscenium. Showing first suburban runs of Rank and Gaumont, closure in December 1961 was for conversion to Top Rank bingo.

The name is blanked in this 1972 view. Now demolished.

THE CAPITOL OVERTON STREET EDGE HILL

Built for the talkies, this 1585 seater 'super' opened in 1930. Showing later runs, even Cinemascope in 1958 and a film plus bingo programme failed to prevent closure in December 1961.

copyright Reflections www.20thcenturyimages.co.uk

A 1962 view of the closed Capitol. (above) The interior is when newly built. After closure, Freemans used it as a warehouse, but by the end of 1963 an Ambassador Ten Pin Bowling had taken its place, as seen on the next page.

CAPITOL OVERTON STREET EDGE HILL continued

Freemans used it as a store, as seen in this Christmas 1962 shot, but it was demolished in January 1963 for construction of a new store with Ambassador Ten Pin Bowling on the ground floor, well on in April.

Copyright images, Freeman Family Archive.

THE CARLTON CINEMA MOSS LANE ORRELL PARK
Orrell Park Picture House Ltd built and owned it all its cinema life.

Seating 1550, it opened in September 1930. Cinemascope was installed in 1955, but masked down, due to the narrow proscenium.

Showing later runs, it survived until February 1974, now a bingo club

1931 views and advert.

THE CARLTON THEATRE GREEN LANE TUEBROOK

ABC opened this 1925 seater in June 1932, another Shennan design.

LIVERPOOL POST AND MERCURY, FRIDAY, JUNE 10, 1932

The Carlton Theatre Opens

Liverpool's Latest Accommodates 2,000 People

CARLTON THEATRE · TUEBROOK

SUMPTUOUS CAFE
SPACIOUS CAR PARK

LIVERPOOL'S LUXURY PICTURE HOUSE

MONDAY, JULY 25th, for THREE DAYS—
BY SPECIAL REQUEST
VIVIENNE SEGAL and WALTER PIDGEON
IN

VIENNESE NIGHTS

CHILDREN ADMITTED.

THURSDAY, JULY 28th, for THREE DAYS—
WILLIAM POWELL and EVELYN BRENT, in

HIGH PRESSURE

CHILDREN ADMITTED.

ABC built a ten pin bowling alley on the car park, after the short lived craze it became the 'Coconut Grove' nightclub. In 1972, a 'Painted Wagon' bar was made in the stalls, leaving only the balcony. Closed in 1982. In the derelict auditorium, you can see that the screen was brought forward of the original proscenium on a scaffolding frame.

Foyer, James Bell at the organ and a plaster relief stag on the stalls wall.

THE CLUBMOOR PICTURE HOUSE TOWNSEND LANE

This is the front page of the Walton Times, proclaiming the opening on 31 October 1925. Seating 1000 in a stadium type auditorium, it was owned all its cinema life by the same company that had the New Premier on Prescot Road.

No canopy was provided, due to the adequate internal waiting rooms.

The narrow proscenium did not preclude the installation of Cinemascope in 1955, though it is not known if the screen was erected forwards of the arch. Films were late runs of the circuit releases, mixed with off-circuit ones.

Above, 2009 shot, only the roof gives a clue.

Closure came on July 2 1960. The building was first converted into a supermarket, but the present use is as a day nursery. All traces of its cinema past have gone.

THE COLISEUM CITY ROAD WALTON

Opened in December 1922, there were 978 seats, including a balcony. Part of ABC from 1936, it showed late runs and re-issues. Despite a new proscenium and Cinemascope in 1955, it closed on 1 December 1956. For decades it was Everton Supporters Club, painted blue (what else?), but is currently a nightclub and function suite, with the balcony as one suite, whilst the stalls has the stage.

1953 Coronation

The original proscenium, seen here in 1954, before Cinemascope.

THE COLISEUM LINACRE ROAD LITHERLAND

Sharing some features with the Regent, Crosby, A. E. Shennan designed this 1442 seater, which opened in February 1921.

ESSOLDO CINEMA LITHERLAND
SUNDAY, 11th NOVEMBER, 1962
Special **BINGO** Attraction
Plus FASHION SHOW by
"ROSALIND"
of Litherland
152, Linacre Road.   Tel. Bootle 5391.
Plus
JILLPOT AND LUCKY NUMBERS

Doors Open 7-15   Commence 8 p.m.
ADMISSION 2/- — BINGO CARDS 4/-
20 Games

We Wish an Enjoyable Evening to all Members.

Photos from 1986, post fire. Sound chamber and the proscenium are revealed inside

Became Essoldo in 1954, the new owners spending £20,000 on Cinemascope, redecoration and improvements. A bingo hall in 1963, as the Coliseum again, ending in 1983 after a serious fire. The destroyed false ceiling exposed original features.

THE COMMODORE STANLEY ROAD KIRKDALE

Regent Enterprises built this 1881 seater in 1930, under ABC the following year.

1967, almost at the end of its cinema voyage!

Screening first suburban runs. Cinemascope was installed in 1955. Closed November 1968 for bingo A proscenium width of 54 feet and an original screen size of 34 x 22 feet, it was the largest in Lancashire, with 120ft throw. From 1982 a funeral director's and then a car parts store, now self storage after total reconstruction internally. Only the facade remains, a rather sad reminder of the past!

THE CORONA CINEMA COLLEGE ROAD CROSBY

Gaumont owned from 1928 but built in 1920 with 1112 seats latterly. One of the first circuit casualties, closing in December 1956

R. Costain &Sons had almost finished building in 1920 and below left after opening.

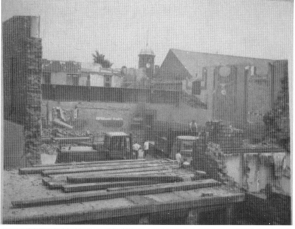

Rainfords have also almost finished, but in this case demolishing it in the 1960's. The girder supported the balcony front.

The only clue to its location today, is the 'Corona Buildings' row of shops.

The CORONA CROSBY

NOVEMBER 1938

Telephone: CROSBY 762.

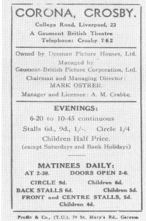

CORONA, CROSBY.

College Road, Liverpool, 23
A Gaumont British Theatre
Telephone: Crosby 762

Owned by Denman Picture Houses, Ltd.
Managed by
Gaumont-British Picture Corporation, Ltd.
Chairman and Managing Director:
MARK OSTRER.
Manager and Licensee: A. M. Crabbe.

EVENINGS:
6-20 to 10-45 continuous
Stalls 6d., 9d., 1/-.   Circle 1/4
Children Half Price.
(except Saturdays and Bank Holidays)

MATINEES DAILY:
AT 2-30.   DOORS OPEN 2-0.
CIRCLE 9d.   Children 6d.
BACK STALLS 6d.   Children 5d.
FRONT and CENTRE STALLS, 5d.
Children 4d.

Profit & Co., (T.U.) 74 St. Mary's Rd., Garston

THE CURZON PRESCOT ROAD OLD SWAN

Bedford Cinemas(1928) Ltd opened this 1750 seater stadium in October 1936, the New Regent opposite opened the following year!

Cinemascope in 1954 enabled the Fox output to be shown, but patronage declined It closed on 20 August 1960 and was converted to retail units, split vertically.

THE DERBY PICTUREDROME SCOTLAND ROAD
For the history, please see the case study.

This 2011 shot shows the frontage clearly. You can see the original church gable end, with the 1911 addition in front. The 1929 extension is splayed out at the rear. The auditorium from the projection room. This shows the hangings and frame for Whitneys false ceiling, the funeral directors partitioning ceilings. The arch is the beginning of the 1929 extension.

A very long throw to the screen from the projection room, unseen for 48 years! Exposed is the emergency exit door from the projection room., with cladding removal.

DINGLE PICTUREDROME PARK ROAD

DINGLE PICTUREDROME,

TO-DAY (WEDNESDAY),
THE

Daily Courier

Presents an Interesting Novel Film
Story :

"THE BIRTH OF A BIG DAILY."

Opened in 1912, with 850 seats, it was part of a small circuit, which sold out to Denman Picture Houses in 1928 (effectively Gaumont British), and closed in 1929, not being worth installing sound. The company already had the Rivoli and Beresford nearby. Demolished in 1935 to build the Gaumont.

The architects, Campbell & Fairhurst, designed the Lido, Belmont Road and the Picturehouse in Stafford to the same design, the latter still exists as a public house(Right) They still show pictures....with a drink!

THE EMPRESS WEST DERBY ROAD TUEBROOK

With 915 seats it was a typical suburban hall, built in 1915. Under Gaumont from 1928, despite the ABC Carlton, it survived until 1960.

Rebuilt front for supermarket in 1966. Demolished 1967, road widening

EVENING EXPRESS—Friday, September 2, 1955

DID NOT LIKE LIVERPOOL, FIRED CINEMA SAY POLICE

15-year-old boy accused

WHEN he could not open the door of the office at the Empress Cinema, West Derby-road, Tuebrook, a 15-year-old boy, who said he did not like Liverpool "got mad," and started a fire which did about £2,000 worth of damage.

This was alleged by Mr. A. Evans, prosecuting, at Liverpool Juvenile Court, today, when the boy was remanded in custody until Monday.

The boy, who is from West Hartlepool, was accused of stealing from the cinema shop, 400 cigarettes, ten lolly ices and a box of matches, total value £3 7s. 2d., and of "eaking out of the shop.

The property belonged to the Circuit Management Association Ltd.

He was also accused of maliciously setting fire to the cinema, and of breaking into a shop in Stanley-road and stealing 5,240 cigarettes, ten-dozen pairs of nylons and other property, total value £88 5s. 2d., property of James Ronald Brown.

Mr. Evans said that on August 21 two boys, one of them the boy before the court, absconded from a hostel in Liverpool. The other boy was arrested on August 27 and had been remanded in custody until next Monday on a charge of shop-breaking.

The boy before the court, said Mr. Evans, had made a statement considered an admission of the offence of arson and also of other offences.

Mr. Evans alleged that the boy said he did not like Liverpool and decided to set the cinema on fire. He put cardboard cartons and paper under the screen curtains and set the screen alight.

Only excellent work by the whole Fire Service saved the building from becoming a total loss.

When charged with stealing from the cinema shop the boy said: "I only stole two ice-lollies. To the arson charge he said: "I did do that, sir." He denied taking the nylons.

After the boy had promised not to abscond again, he was sent to a remand home.

You could not make this one up, could you?

This is just one example of the targeting of cinemas by petty thieves. The lure was always cash and cigarettes and sometimes a fire was started to cover their tracks. Unlike today, alarms were fitted only to the managers office, where the safe was, so the rest of the building was accessible, usually by breaking a window, which police foot patrols would discover.

This is just one example

THE EVERTON PALACE HEYWORTH STREET EVERTON

An independent with 900 seats, 1912 marked its opening. Showing later runs, it was one of the second wave of closures in March 1960

A 1912 view of the ornate facade. The auditorium was behind.
Maurice Friedman, British Music Hall Society.

Not the biggest betting shop in the world, but the auditorium of the Palace in 1966. Rays Glass and China were using it as a warehouse, having demolished the front part for access.

The remains were finally demolished as part of the 1960's Rupert Lane Clearance Area

THE FORUM LIME STREET

Built by ABC and designed by their architect, W. R. Glen. With 1835 seats, this super cinema gave the company its prime city centre site.

1959 shot, with the doomed Palais de Luxe Just visible at the end of the block.

This allowed closure of the Olympia and ceasing to operate the Prince of Wales, Clayton Square. Opened in May 1931, it was tripled in 1982, final closure, due to declining patronage, was in 1998

The interior in 1931. Note the very narrow proscenium.

The grand reopening after tripling, was in August 1983. Now named just the ABC. A new widescreen was installed forward of the proscenium, serving the former circle and two screens in the stalls were created.

Now Grade 2 listed, the building survives unused, to date, although there was recent activity within for asbestos removal and a lot of skips full of breeze blocks.

THE FUTURIST LIME STREET

Opened as the Picture House in 1912, with 1029 seats. Part of the Levy circuit, Birmingham from 1920, renamed Futurist. Leased by Fox from 1954 to 1960 for their Cinemascope films, then under ABC for roadshow movies. Closed July 1982

Equipment moved to the tripled Forum.

1938 facade (above)
1954 inside('Scope)
1961 new projectors

1982 front and the foyer in 1944

THE GAIETY CINEMA SCOTLAND ROAD

Edwin Haigh, who had the Derby further up, then built this, opening in May 1915. Long and narrow, yet about 1000 capacity. Showing later circuit runs, it lasted until 14 May 1960, the Derby closing also.

Tatty in the 1950's, then derelict, less display board

THE GEM VESCOCK STREET VAUXHALL

Opened August 1926 and under ABC from 1936. A stadium type, seating 1350. Noted for its terrible acoustics, it became run down and closed in February 1958. Subsequently used as St Sylvesters social club before demolition as part of a clearance area. The council later named a street "Gem" in memory of the cinema.

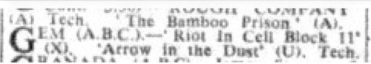

Already past its use by date in 1982, looking little better in 1967. These are the type of tired and not very comfortable halls which were soon deserted for the telly!

THE GAINSBOROUGH KNOWSLEY ROAD BOOTLE

Seating 1311 it opened in 1922, under ABC from 1931 and closed in 1960. Re-opened as a bingo club, the site is now a garage.

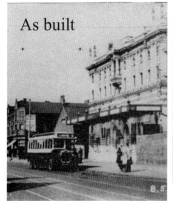

As built

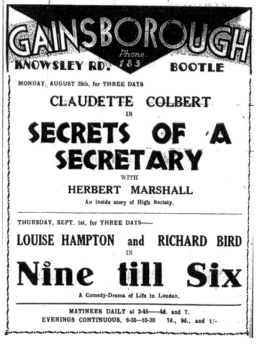

By 1985 the facade had lost much of its ornamentation and the canopy! Demolished 2001.

Hurt your eyes, 1985 'bingo coloured' interior. Note the rear stalls has become a bar. Original seating still in the balcony.

THE GARRICK, WESTMINSTER ROAD, KIRKDALE

Dating from 1916, it lasted until 1959, despite the nearby Astoria.

This became a typical flea pit, being taken over by Essoldo in 1954, when they aquired the Southan Morris Circuit. The middle two pictures are from November 1962
By this time it had been vandalised, but due to the insatiable demand for bingo, it was repaired and enjoyed a reprieve from the wreckers ball for a few years!

GARRICK, Westminster Rd.
'THE CHARGE IS MURDER' (A).
Charles Banel, 'Sicilian Story' (U).
GAUMONT, Allerton.—Glenn Ford in

This is the bingo club in August 1968.
It closed and was demolished shortly afterwards.
The site is now housing, yet another example of vanishing without a trace!

THE EMPIRE JAMES STREET GARSTON
Originally a cine-variety theatre with 876 seats, opened 1915, (Bedford Cinemas)

2008 view showing the built out projection room, films to 1962, bingo until 2007.

In bingo colours, this 1981 picture shows the horseshoe shaped balcony. The screen could be flown for stage shows and is still there behind the proscenium.

THE EMPIRE JAMES STREET GARSTON continued

Another 1981 showing the seating, unchanged from a cinema.

The balcony has been isolated by a false ceiling and extensive modernisation obliterates most decorations, taken after closure.

THE GAUMONT PALACE OAKFIELD ROAD ANFIELD

On the site of the Kings Hall cinema, opened December 1931 with 1600 seats. It had a 40 foot proscenium, stage and dressing rooms. Showing 2nd run Gaumont suburban releases, it lasted until 1960.

Liverpool Lighthouse have restored the art-deco interior, extending the balcony to create a hall. Amazing that so much survived industrial use!

The original proscenium, now hidden behind a curtained area.

THE GAUMONT PALACE ANFIELD continued

1931 and above in 1948

Up for sale in 1961. Appletons bought it for their hardware warehouse

THE GAUMONT STANLEY ROAD BOOTLE

Replacing the bombed Broadway, post war restrictions delayed building until 1955. A stadium type with 1350 seats, it cost Rank £120,000 and had a reinforced concrete barrel vaulted roof, one of only two in the country. Re-named Odeon, April 1964, closed 1975, an indoor skateboard park before its present use as a snooker hall.

As Rileys 2009, note completed roof.

THE GAUMONT PARK ROAD DINGLE

On the site of the Dingle Picturedrome, it opened in March 1937. With 1500 seats, it lasted until September 1966, when converted into a Top Rank Bingo club. Closed, replaced by the Mecca and a failed attempt to convert it into a community venue.

See also the case study, which illustrates the politics involved.

GAUMONT, Prince's Park (Mat. 1.45, Cont. 5.30)—' ROUGH COMPANY ' (A) Tech. ' The Bamboo Prison ' (A). GEM (A.B.C.).—' Riot In Cell Block 11'

BINGO AT THE TOP RANK CLUB, Princes Park. All seats sold for Grand Opening to-night (Thursday), October 13. Normal sessions from to-morrow, Friday, October 14. Join Now.

* BINGO

THE GROSVENOR, STANLEY ROAD.

PRESENTS

BONANZA NIGHT

TOMORROW, FRIDAY, OCT. 14.

SECOND SESSION GUARANTEED

£50 PER HOUSE

DOORS OPEN 7 p.m.
EYES DOWN 8.15 p.m.

BINGO AT THE TOP RANK CLUB, Princes Park. All seats sold for Grand Opening to-night (Thursday), October 13. Normal sessions from to-morrow, Friday, October 14. Join Now.

MECCA OLYMPIA CASINO
WEST DERBY ROAD, LIVERPOOL 6
Announcing for To-morrow Night
A BEST DRESSED TRAMP CONTEST
WITH A FIRST PRIZE OF £5
Also meet FRED SPROCKETT, the oldest tramp in the business, on his annual John o' Groats to Land's End Marathon walk plus, of course,
BIG TIME BINGO FOR BIG TIME PRIZES
Doors open 6.30 p.m.   Eyes down 8 p.m.

BIG NEWS . . . . Top Rank Bingo, Princes Park (formerly the Gaumont). Grand opening to-night at 7.45 p.m.

THE GRANADA EAST PRESCOT ROAD DOVECOT

Seating 1803 and opened in 1932, ABC aquired it in 1935. Showing first suburban releases. Bingo from 1961.

After Mecca built new premises, it became a community centre and pub, with a boxing ring upstairs, with the original balcony and seats looking out on it.

THE GRAND SMITHDOWN ROAD ALLERTON

With an ornate frontage, this was built in 1913, seating 824. Under Gaumont ownership from 1928, it was one of their first closures in September 1956, despite Cinemascope being installed in 1955.

Silent era flyer

The interior in 1922, long and narrow. Nothing 'grand' about the Fallowfield Road side, the residents must have been glad to be rid!
The present day site. The 'Grand' petrol station was the first occupant, now a used car dealership.
After closure, posters for films at the Odeon, Allerton Road were exhibited!

THE GRAPHIC CINEMA BOALER STREET

This was a small cinema, seating 630, including a small balcony. Opening in 1922, it was re-named the Cosy ten years later. Screening later runs, closure was on 4 January 1958 It was used as a meat packers, who put a false ceiling in, then furniture storage.
The building has now been renovated, mezzanine floor inserted for its use as a church centre.

Removal of the spiral stairs meant no access to the projection room. During the alterations, the original neon sign was found in there!

THE GROSVENOR STANLEY ROAD KIRKDALE

A 1922 stadium type seating 1040. Four owners, Essoldo being the last from 1954 to closure in August 1963. Bingo lasted until 1995 .

Top Flight Bingo colours on the front in 1981.

BINGO

THE GROSVENOR, STANLEY ROAD.

PRESENTS

BONANZA NIGHT

TOMORROW. FRIDAY. OCT. 14.

SECOND SESSION GUARANTEED

£50 PER HOUSE

DOORS OPEN 7 p.m.
EYES DOWN 8.15 p.m.

2010 interior view as funeral directors,   Bingo pictures from 1985

THE HOMER GREAT HOMER STREET

Licensed in 1914, it had 950 seats, including balcony. Aquired by Essoldo as part of the Southan Morris circuit in 1954, but not renamed. Restricted to later runs, it closed in January 1962.

The cinema is behind the war damaged block, 1950

A 1966 view of the facade.

!967 and the building next door has gone, The side elevation is on Kew Street. Demolished shortly afterwards, for redevelopment.

HOMER, Gt. Homer St.—Rock Hudson, Jane Wyman in 'Magnificent Obsession' (U). Supporting programme. Cont. 6 p.m.

The only advertising was in the "Echo".

HOPE HALL CINEMA HOPE STREET

Built in 1837 as Hope Hall Chapel, a public hall from 1853 and in 1915 became a cinema. Showing late runs, it survived until 1959 but re-opened for two further years in 1961 as the Everyman Cinema.

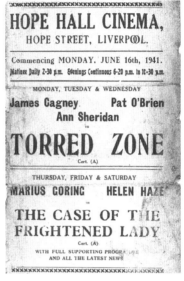

1941 handbill
All 960 seats could be filled!

Late 1930's view towards Mount Pleasant

Above view after the first closure in 1959 The 1961 advert is for the short lived revival, re-named Everyman in December.

The next use was the Everyman Theatre, which re-built most of the building in 1977 and was demolished in 2011 to be rebuilt larger.

THE SUN HALL STANLEY ROAD BOOTLE

Originally built as a gospel hall, in 1906 it became Bootles first proper cinema. Renamed the Imperial Cinema from 1923, major improvements in 1930 resulted in a 40 foot wide proscenium. The same syndicate also owned the nearby Palace and both had to show late runs and B movies. Despite Cinemascope, it closed in March 1959.

By the mid-1960's, the foyer was in use as a shop, whilst the main hall fell into dereliction. Note the hall at a right angle behind. Now the site of a new bingo hall.

THE ELECTRA PALACE THEATRE LONDON ROAD

Originally a stadium type theatre, a cinematograph licence was granted in 1911. Renamed the Alhambra in 1920. Following refurbishment and the addition of a balcony in 1932 it was now the Kings. In 1957 it became the Essoldo, later the Curzon, Classic and finally the Eros Club. Closed by the council in August 1981, for showing uncensored films. Demolished May 1994.

1984, closed, Essoldo removed the canopy in 1967.

Two views after refurbishment in 1932. Note the very narrow music hall type proscenium.

THE LIDO BELMONT ROAD ANFIELD

The Belmont Road Picture House, with 717 seats, opened January 1914. Renamed in 1938, it lasted until June 1959. Same facade design as the Dingle Picturedrome.

1965, as a NEMS depot. Later as Wookey Hollow Club.

Closed after a 1982 fire, site now occupied by a kitchen firm.

THE LYCEUM ST MARYS ROAD GARSTON

With 800 seats, this opened in December 1922. A long narrow hall with a 17 ft. wide proscenium A widescreen was installed in 1953, but it closed in 1959.

Currently a garage, but very little left of its past, except the ceiling.

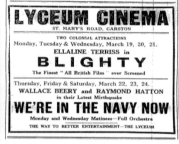

THE LIVERPOOL PICTURE HOUSE CLAYTON SQUARE

Opened 1912 on the site of the Prince of Wales theatre. Seating 700, it had several name changes, including the Liverpool News Theatre. But the Jacey, from 1963 -72.

January 1958, but still Christmas!

It became The Shrine of The Blessed Sacrament until demolition in 1986 for the Clayton Square redevelopment

THE LIVERPOOL PICTURE HOUSE, continued.

The auditorium, when reconstructed as a cinema.

THE LYRIC THEATRE EVERTON VALLEY

This 1897 built theatre was re-named The Lyric Super Cinema in 1922 showing films until 1925, when it reverted to a theatre.

Closed by the fire brigade in 1932, due to exits not up to standard. Bombed during the war, Rainfords Demolition used it as a yard. The remains in 1970 with cropped 'ghost' sign advertising performances! Next to the opening was a bricked up door headed "Stage Door", which lasted until demolition (good paint!).

THE LYTTON CINEMA LYTTON STREET EVERTON

Opening as the Princes Picture Palace in 1911, it was a stadium type with 600 seats. Re-named in 1918, it remained an independent, Cinemascope being installed in 1955, but closing four years later.

Very little on this one, even advertising was rarely used.
Left, April 1970 as cigar importers.

Above, site in 2011, below, May 1955 ad

THE MAGNET PICTON ROAD WAVERTREE

Licence granted December 1914, this 1038 seater stadium type became a Gaumont theatre in 1928, showing first suburban runs. Despite the nearby Abbey, it survived until May 1959.

This 1970 view shows it as a warehouse., but the facade is much the same as its cinema days. It is set well back from Picton Road,.

This later shot shows it cut down for use as a squash club, before disappearing!

THE MAJESTIC PICTURE HOUSE DAULBY STREET

Opened in 1914 with 870 seats, in 1927 increased to 1109 by the removal of waiting rooms either side of the front auditorium. Plans were approved for a larger super cinema in 1937 and it closed on April 3rd, being immediately demolished.

The tower is similar to the one on the Palladium, West Derby Road.
The architect is unknown, unfortunately

This rare interior shot shows the lack of rake to the stalls and their front extension. Just visible are the cast iron columns supporting the balcony.

THE MAJESTIC DAULBY STREET

This 1794 seater opened in 1937 replacing a smaller cinema, the original Majestic. Always an independent, Cinemascope was installed in 1954 and it closed in June 1970, the site being a compulsory purchase required for the new Royal Hospital. Note the offset auditorium.

1966 STAFF LINE UP
George Stevenson, Operator
Bryan Collings, Manager
Alice Morgan, Front of House
Leslie Ward, Doorman

THE MAYFAIR DERBY ROAD HUYTON

Opening in September 1937, seating 676 in the stalls/333 in the balcony

Films shown were a mixture of late releases and 'off circuit' B pictures. Latterly, so many westerns were shown that it was nicknamed 'The Ranch'
Closed in 1960 after only 23 years, the building still survives as a Boots The Chemist, rebuilt at both ends, so not obvious what it originally was!

'PRINCE' (U), Colour, C.Scope, Car Park,
MAYFAIR, Huyton.—Rock Hudson in
'TAZA, SON OF COCHISE' (U)
Tech, Shelley Winters, 'Playgirl' 7.45 only
MERE LANE—Glenn Ford, 'HUMAN

THE MAYFAIR SUPER CINEMA AIGBURTH ROAD

Opened in May 1937, by Bedford Cinemas(1928) Ltd. Boasting 1750 seats, it was in direct competition with the Gaumont halls on each side

The 'Lenscrete' canopy is shown top right This let daylight through.

Showing mainly ABC releases, a giant 'floating' screen replaced the proscenium in 1969. Closed in 1973 then Mecca bingo until 1984.

" The Last Picture Show" was the final film shown. This is the remake, as it becomes rubble in 1986.

Site now occupied by shops, the cinema only existing in memories.....

THE MERE LANE SUPER CINEMA MERE LANE EVERTON

Opened in 1918 with 1050 seats, it ended up under Essoldo in 1954. Cinemascope was installed in 1955, finally closing in September 1963, for bingo.

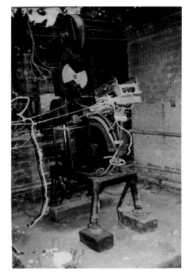

Projector still there
1981 exterior in Top Flight Bingo colours. Originally there was a glass canopy.
As a 1980's club. Balcony floor extended, merman on proscenium (original?) but the stepped ceiling has been retained and restored.

Ornate columns in the former entrance, super for its day.
A fire in the 1990's destroyed a lot and reinstated with a false ceiling.
Presently derelict and vandalised, a mere shell If it wasn't for the mobile phone masts it would have been demolished.!

THE METROPOLE THEATRE STANLEY ROAD BOOTLE

Opening in February 1911, seating 1850, it was converted to cine-variety in August 1931. Not a success, it reverted to a live theatre, but 3 days later was destroyed in an air raid on 7 May 1941

THE ROYAL MUNCASTER THEATRE IRLAM ROAD BOOTLE

Former music hall built 1890, converted to the Strand cinema in 1921. A warehouse for Cork Industries Ltd after its 1948 closure, burnt down 1964 after being burgled.

May 1822 Ad

The End In July 1964

THE MOULTON PICTURE PALACE ROSCOMMON STREET

A conversion of the public Moulton Hall in 1910. Seating 700, heating was by open fires! Modernised and renamed the Tivoli in 1920 (with a new heating system!). Part of a small independent circuit, it was the first post-war Liverpool closure in January 1954.

ROUGH SKETCH.   INTERIOR OF HALL

Rough Sketch of Exterior as Suggested.

Elevation to Roscommon Street.

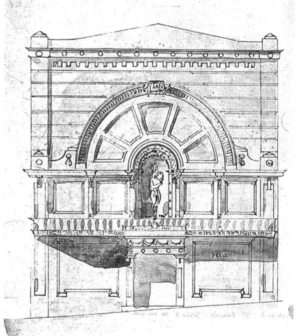

No photographs have been traced, so these drawings are the only record of what it looked like.

THE NEW ADELPHI CINEMA CHRISTIAN STREET

The original Adelphi Theatre opened in 1846 and showed films between 1911 and 1921. A larger purpose built cinema was then built further along Christian Street, with 1134 seats, opened in 1922. Very plain frontage for the time.

Note the shop stuffed into the corner! Bomb damaged in 1941 and later demolished.

The site in 1967, before the present road system

THE NEW CENTURY HALL, MOUNT PLEASANT

Converted from a Wesleyan chapel in 1908, it was the first city cinema. Under Gaumont control from 1928 and closed a year later.

The church windows show its origin, a 1959 view from the Adelphi Hotel roof.

After being auction room and a carpet warehouse, the final use was the "Mardi Gras" jazz club, demolished 1970's. Who remembers the Bee? They had a shop on Renshaw Street as well.

CENTURY THEATRE.
MOUNT PLEASANT (LIVERPOOL'S REPERTORY CINEMA).
THE HOME OF UNUSUAL FILMS
TODAY
"KEAN,"
Based on Alex. Dumas' Play of the same name.
Featuring
IVAN MOSJUKINE.
Approx. Times: 2.40, 4.50, 7.0, 9.5.
TOMORROW (SAT.), March 2nd. for Six Days,
"THE STUDENT OF PRAGUE,"
Featuring
CONRAD VEIDT and
WERNER KRAUSS.
Approx. Times for Saturday Only:
2.0, 3.45, 5.35, 7.25, 9.5.

1967

THE NEW COLISEUM PADDINGTON

Opened in 1889 as a music hall, in 1910 it was converted to a cinema by the pioneering Weisker brothers. Seating 650 it became part of ABC from 1935. Cinemascope was installed in October 1955, but it was one of the first closures, on 6 December 1956. Demolished 1960s

Its the canopy at the top of Paddington.

Two interiors from the 1950's Typical music hall decorations and proscenium.

THE NEW PREMIER PRESCOT ROAD OLD SWAN

Built 1912, the same company also owned the Clubmoor. An early 1000 seater stadium, showing later releases and off-circuits. Lasting until 1959, only the set back auditorium remains, latterly as a bar.

Facade, rebuilt in 1950's

In 1955, a fire occurred, destroying the screen, as seen below. Note the loudspeakers.

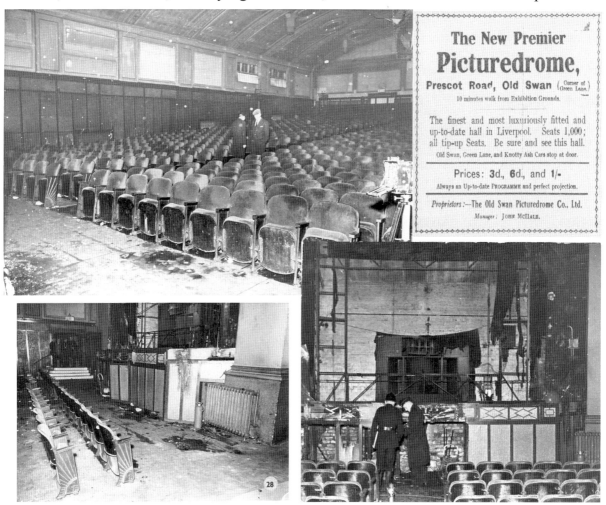

The New Premier
Picturedrome,
Prescot Road, Old Swan (Corner of Green Lane.)
10 minutes walk from Exhibition Grounds.

The finest and most luxuriously fitted and up-to-date hall in Liverpool. Seats 1,000; all tip-up Seats. Be sure and see this hall.
Old Swan, Green Lane, and Knotty Ash Cars stop at door.

Prices: 3d., 6d., and 1/-
Always an Up-to-date PROGRAMME and perfect projection.

Proprietors:—The Old Swan Picturedrome Co., Ltd.
Manager: JOHN McHALE.

NEW REGENT PRESCOT ROAD OLD SWAN
A 1724 seater to replace the Regent next door, opened in 1938.

Architect, W. R. Glen

ABC owned, it showed Gaumont/ Rank releases. Competing with the Curzon opposite, until 1960, a revamp in 1962 only bought it 5 more years. Promptly demolished, Baden House is now on the site. The offset entrance was in Baden Road. View from roof in 1951. The Curzon is prominent (competition!)

TWINNING THE ODEON LONDON ROAD

This was the first twin cinemas (in an existing building) in the North West. Opening on 20 March 1969, the cost was £340,000.

As a lot of patrons still liked to go once a week, when the Odeon was clogged up for months with a roadshow then they would have to go elsewhere! This was the solution, having 2 screens, one for long runs.

Sadly, the original ceiling and decorations were not retained.

Gutted to a shell, Odeon 1 was formed upstairs with 1989 seats and utilising the existing projection room. A new licensed bar was also created on this level, converted in 1979 to a 148 seater Odeon 5. Increasing the number of screens, made it possible to close the Gaumont.

These pictures show the Odeon 1 with its arched design and the new bar, designed for rapid service.

TWINNING THE ODEON LONDON ROAD continued

Odeon 2 had 1405 seats and was downstairs. With a flat, low ceiling and no proscenium. A new projection room was built at the rear. This had Cinemation to automatically run the show, a later working version of Essoldo's 'Projectormatic'

Cinemation unit

Colour coding was used to identify each screen. Odeon 1 was red and 2 was blue. Starting at the readograph outside, the colours continued, showing a route to the right screen. Even the toilets were colour coded! Air conditioning was provided throughout. The 'Paramount' facade and canopy disappeared under galvanised steel ribbed sheets.

Once more screens were created, the concept was lost due to sub-division, with screens created all over the place!

The art-deco balcont stairs handrails were boxed in and thus survived until demolition. Where are they now?

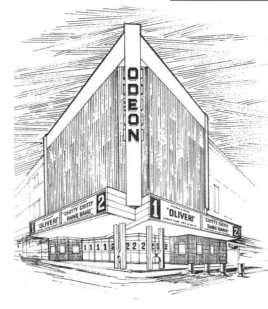

THE OLYMPIA WEST DERBY ROAD

A Frank Matcham designed 3750 seat theatre of 1905. Became a cinema in 1925, leased by ABC in 1929 and closed March 1939.

The first 'talkie' in Liverpool, from 11 February 1929 filled it! Later the Mecca Locarno from 1949, bingo after 1964 and its present use as a venue for events. The 1980 view of bingo is taken from the gallery, now curtained off.

Frank Matcham's Listed riot of detailing, shown how it looks today. The Gallery is curtained off to save on heating bills!

THE PALACE WARBRECK MOOR AINTREE

With 960 seats, it was opened in November 1913. Owned by the Aintree Picture Palace Co. Ltd, this stadium type had Cinemascope in 1955, but closed in June 1959. Present use is a supermarket.

As built, a canopy was later added, seen in 1952,
Then a plain brick front in 1954. Lennons in 1979

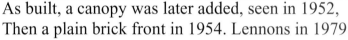

The Palace, Aintree
Tel.: WALTON 50.

Monday to Friday. Continuous Performance from 6-30. Saturdays and Holidays, Two Houses, 6-30 and 8-40. Matinees—Daily at 2-45 p.m.

MONDAY, FEB. 23rd. for THREE DAYS—

GREAT ATTRACTIONS ALL THIS WEEK

RICHARD BARTHELMESS,
CONSTANCE BENNETT and DOROTHY MATTHEWS in

SON OF THE GODS

"East is East and West is West"—but the twain meet in "Son of the Gods."

THURSDAY, FEB. 26th, for THREE DAYS—

100 STARS —— 1,000 BEAUTIES in

SHOW OF SHOWS

100 SHOWS IN ONE.

Amazing—Thrilling—Astounding! The Greatest Entertainment the Screen has ever known.

THE PALACE MARSH LANE BOOTLE

Opening in 1912, with 1,000 seats, it showed later runs and survived until 1958. It then became Bootle Social Centre, lasting about another 40 years until demolition for an access road.

The rebuilt frontage   The interior, the ceiling is visible

THE PICTURE PALACE OF BOOTLE KNOWSLEY ROAD

Erected in 1882 as the Bootle Institute and became a cinema in 1908. Re-named the Empire in 1912, closure came in 1922, with the opening of the Gainsborough across the road. It still survives as a club.

Inside, there were basic roof trusses, but the facade is so ornate

THE PALAIS DE LUXE LIME STREET

Formerly the Grand Tivoli Music Hall, films began to be shown from 1908. It was the last city cinema to install sound in August 1930.
Unsuitable for Cinemascope, despite modernisation it closed in 1959.

A 1950 view of the facade

In 1959 it is on the left

The fire in June 1951

The narrow proscenium and Musicians gallery.

The Cameraman

Exterior in 1955, a plain and modern style.
Above, close-up of the metal cameraman motif.
Left, Removal during demolition. What happened to it?

THE PALLADIUM SEAFORTH ROAD SEAFORTH

Another of Shennans designs, 1913 saw the opening of this 905 seater. An independant, it closed in 1959 and is now Grade 2 Listed

PALLADIUM
SEAFORTH ROAD.
FRONT STALLS 4D., BACK STALLS 6D., BALCONY 9D.
(Matinee 2d.)
Including Tax.

Matinees 3 p.m.   Evening 6.30 to 10.30 p.m.
Daily   Continuous

The restored balcony front, but with a gym behind it. The original ceiling is still above the false one. The original glass canopy is seen above, pure 'picture palace' style.

The staff pose on the stage in 1951. Just to run a small cinema took this many people!

THE PALLADIUM WEST DERBY ROAD

Opened in May, 1913 and having 905 seats, it was always independent.
A real family cinema. It only closed in July 1967 because of a compulsory purchase order for road widening. The manager even took a petition to 10 Downing Street, but to no avail. Demolished the week after it closed!

Above, as in January 1967, too cold for ice cream?
Left, updated proscenium in 1950. The seating has been retained and redecorated throughout.
Last film, the epic "The Ten Commandments"

THE PARAMOUNT THEATRE LONDON ROAD

On the site of a former boxing stadium, this was the largest purpose built cinema in Liverpool, with 2,670 seats, opening in 1934.

In 1959, as the Odeon.

Became an Odeon in 1942, Cinemascope and TODD-AO equipped in the 1950's, twinned in 1968 with all detailing lost. Ended up with 10 screens but closed when Liverpool One opened. Now demolished.

THE PARK PALACE MILL STREET TOXTETH

Built in 1894 as a theatre and changed to pictures and variety in 1908. Under the control of the Dunn family from 1911, the variety gave way to sound in 1930. Seating 960, it lasted until March 1959. Subsequent uses included a works, car parts store and a chemist.

The plain facade in 2009. The name was restored in 2008, when it was used for a play.
Below, The proscenium was only 30 feet wide, yet Cinemascope was installed. We can only assume that the screen was brought forward of the arch. You can see where the circular balcony was by the panelling

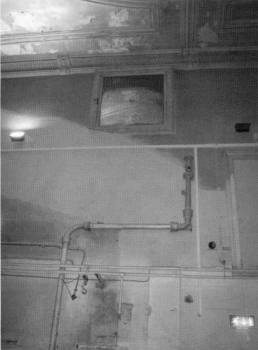

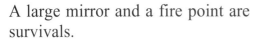

A large mirror and a fire point are survivals.
The ornate ceiling and dome, which would have had gas jets to lift the stale air. The projection room was hung from the rear wall, now removed.

THE PICTUREDROME KENSINGTON

The second purpose built cinema, it opened in 1910 with 1050 seats. Owned by the Liverpool Picturedrome Ltd all its life, it lasted until December 1958. Subsequently a TV repairers, an amusement arcade and currently a public house.

As amusements, less canopy but still with dome

December 2008 and the last rays of the sun catch the dome. Inside it no longer resembles a cinema, but at least the building is not a pile of rubble!

THE PLAZA ALLERTON ROAD ALLERTON

Built in 1928 for the J.F. Wood circuit, it became part of the Gaumont chain in the same year. Another Shennan design seating 1432, unusually with a foyer fountain.

Above Allerton Road from the roof.
Closed as the Classic, 18 April 1971

THE PLAZA ALLERTON, continued

Closure came in April 1971, the large site and car park sold for redevelopment. The facade and interior shots during the last ever performance on 18 April. The left pic is so atmospheric, typical of traditional cinema interiors.
One projector was dismantled as the other ran the final reel!

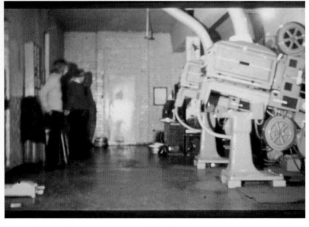

THE PLAZA CROSBY ROAD NORTH CROSBY

Opened 2 September 1939 - and closed as war was declared the next day! Seating 1450, it was aquired by Odeon in 1943 Renamed in 1945. Later under Classic, Cannon and Apollo. before being bought as a community cinema. Tripled in 1976 by constructing two 'boxes' on each side of the stalls. The centre stalls and balcony was the largest screen.

Building it in 1938. The side walls are part built.

Modern view, showing the two 'boxes'.

THE POPULAR NETHERFIELD ROAD EVERTON

Coliseum And Popular Cinemas To Close

The Coliseum, City Road, Walton and the Popular, Netherfield Road, Everton, are two Associated British Cinemas which are to be closed down as an economy on the part of the cinema industry.

The Coliseum closes on December 1 and the Popular the following week. These two cinemas were established in the early 1920's.

Originally economies on Merseyside were restricted to the Rank organisation and a associated companies.

The reason for the new closures is the same—high entertainment tax and increased operating costs.

A spokesman for A.B.C. said that while they would do their best to absorb employees who would become redundant, particularly those with long service, it was inevitable that some would be out of a job.

Left, 1950 street view.

A very plain hall, seating some 1500, dug into the solid rock at the screen end. Built in 1925, ABC aquired it with the Regent circuit in 1932. Showing 2nd run suburban, it was in the 1956 closures.

It was then just left to rot! This 1967 view from Seacombe Street includes the 1964 Methodist Mission. Final demolition must have been a relief for it. The church building was later gutted by fire!

A rare interior from 1953. Underneath were waiting rooms, hence the lack of canopy.
The rear stalls were at first floor level. Hard to imagine how built up was the area full of terraces.

THE PRINCESS SELWYN STREET KIRKDALE

Opened in 1931, this had the balcony over the foyer and waiting rooms, and seating 1420. Under Essoldo from 1958, bingo arrived in October 1966.

Currently derelict, with plans passed for replacement by flats Sold again, by auction in 2012. The building is still extant in January 2013.

Above, 2007 view from Brewster Street. This is the 'thick end of the wedge', containing staff areas, projection suite and the semi- circular foyer/waiting area.

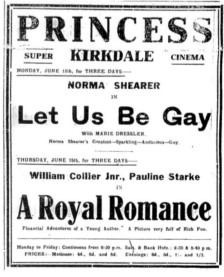

PRINCES, GRANBY STREET, TOXTETH
Converted from the Granby Hall, (billiards) in 1912. Closed Feb 1965

This was a cheap and cheerful conversion, merely grafting a facade onto the existing building. The hall type of building is well illustrated in the side view. Seating was only 600, including a balcony. To Essoldo with the SM circuit in 1954. Derelict by these March 1968 pictures. The scallies get into every empty building, hence the missing windows!
Not a trace remains now.

PRINCE'S, Granby St—Johnny Weiss-
muller, 'JUNGLE MOON MEN' (U)
Plus 'Sagtnan Trail' (U)
QUEEN'S Walton—Iean Simmons In

Cinema index from 11 May 1955, about the only adverts for it.

PROPOSED, NOT BUILT

There were many plans for cinemas, to cope with the publics insatiable appitite for moving pictures. Lack of permissions and/or finance led to them not getting built.

THE ELITE PICTURE PALACE

These buildings in Norton Street were draped with banners proclaiming that they were the site for a new cinema in 1922. Nothing further transpired and the site was finally redeveloped with shops.

Norton Street became the place were the film distributors were based.

Bedford Cinemas has plans for a 'super' cinema in Breeze Hill, Walton. The artists impression above was as far as it got!

A. E. Shennan had this 'stock' drawing, shown on the right. It was used for several proposals, none of which were built like that! The Palladium at Seaforth, is named at the bottom, but built differently.

THE QUEENS PICTURE HOUSE WALTON ROAD

The licence was granted in February 1913, for this stadium type 1200 seater. The capacity was reduced to 960 in 1930, when the screen was moved forward, to facilitate the speakers for sound. One of Wirral Picturedromes Queens circuit, despite competition, it lasted until 1959

The Queens in Walton

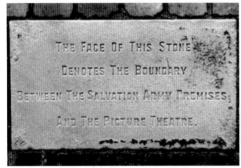

Unusual boundary marker, surviving in 1986. The Salvation Army Hall was demolished also.

It became a supermarket in 1960, then a shop for Clarksons, displaced from Scotland Road but was empty by 1973.

The Co-op's 'modern' front in 1973, Salvation Army right.

Queens

Finally as the Queens Bingo and Social Club, before clearance

THE QUEENS PICTURE HOUSE SOUTH ROAD WATERLOO

Under Wirral Picturedromes Ltd from 1920, this 660 seater was opened in March 1913. Unusually it had no proscenium. Showing second run films, Cinemascope added in 1955, closure came in 1959.

The ornate frontage was rebuilt when it became a furniture shop. Only the roof gives a clue to its past. Inside a first floor has been created. Plans were passed in April 2011 for a public house and shop unit, now extant.

QUEEN'S, Waterloo.—Marilyn Monroe, 'HOW TO MARRY A MILLION-AIRE' (U) Tech. C'Scope. 2.30, 6.45, 9.0.

A 1955 listing in the 'Echo's' cinema index, with the new Cinemascope.

THE REGAL CHURCH ROAD LITHERLAND

With 1046 seats, this stadium type opened in June 1939. Part of ABC from 1955, it closed in July 1962 for conversion to ten pin bowling. After that lost popularity it became a nightclub, now flats on the site.

No real frills on this one! These two shots are from 1939 and as new.
The exterior is simple and functional, with everything inside devoid of lavish decoration.

Inside, there is no proscenium, just a festoon curtain and no decorative plasterwork. The foyer is under the rear stalls.

THE REGAL BROADWAY NORRIS GREEN
Opened 1930 with 1756 seats, under ABC control from 1936.

Apart from Cinemascope installation and a £20k modernisation in 1955, it was unchanged until converted to bingo in October 1964. This lasted until April 2008, the building then being put up for sale, with planning for retail units. Left, middle shots show it in 2011, empty!

Interior and foyer in 1955
Traffic-free Broadway in 1959

THE REGENT LIVERPOOL ROAD CROSBY

An A. E. Shennan design with 1075 seats and opened in 1920. An ABC cinema from 1935, lasting until November 1968, when converted to bingo.

These 1981 interiors show the auditorium plasterwork detailing, albeit in the garish 'bingo' colours. It was 'eyes down' to avoid a colour attack!

Circular waiting room. The same existed at the Coliseum, Litherland (same architect)

THE REGENT CROSBY, continued

The current use is a sports centre.

This was the former cinema cafe

The building still retains a lot of the original features, but the strangest looking is the auditorium, minus the balcony but still with the original ceiling! The ropes would be good for budding Tarzans? Given the current popularity of fitness, this is one building that should survive, even if not as a cinema!

Waiting room detail.

THE REGENT PRESCOT ROAD OLD SWAN

First advertised in 1926, this 1040 seater stadium type was aquired by ABC and closed in 1938, the New Regent replacing it.

After a supermarket, the projection room framing was the only internal feature left, above a false ceiling.

1936 view and 1966 advert

A car showroom from 1959, finally a Kwik-Save. Demolished 2010

THE REO LONGMOOR LANE FAZAKERLEY

With cafe and car park, seating 1508 it opened in January 1933, under ABC from 1936. Screening later runs of the circuits, the nearly 50 foot wide proscenium took Cinemascope in 1955, but damage and disruption by Kirkby patrons hastened its closure in Jan. 1961.

REO (A.B.C.), Fazakerley. — 'THEM' James Whitmore, Edmund Gwenn (X). Also '36 Hours' (A). Dan Duryea. RITZ Utting Ave. — Robert Mitchum in

After dereliction, Mecca refurbished it as a bingo club, which gave it a few more years of life before demolition.

THE RIALTO UPPER PARLIAMENT STREET TOXTETH
Opened in 1927 with 1700 seats plus a ballroom and cafe to boot!

RIALTO   RIALTO

LAST TWO DAYS OF

THE GARDEN OF ALLAH

With ALICE TERRY and IVAN PETROVICH.

Presented with Beautiful Vocal Prologue by

THE SINGERS OF THE EAST.

With Gorgeous Eastern Stage Settings.

AND ALSO ON THE STAGE –

BOB BARLOW,

Character Vocalist.

Watch for the Date of "Q SHIPS."

Under Gaumont (GB) control from 1928. Advert from 1929

In 1953, it hosted the premiere of "Sangaree", the first full length 3D film, using 2 synchronised projectors. Closing February 1964, then a furniture store. Destroyed in 1982 riots

THE RIALTO continued

As Swainbanks furniture store above then the aftermath of the Toxteth riots of 1982! What a way to go!
The current building on the site has reminders of this.

THE RICE LANE PICTURE HOUSE (ATLAS) WALTON

Seating 1000, it opened in May 1914. Renovated in 1932 with less seating and renamed Atlas. Aquired by SM, it passed to Essoldo in 1954. Showing later runs and not well attended, closed March 1958. One of the ultimate in 'flea pits'....eek!

August 1971, 13 years later. Still with canopy to shelter bus queues!
Empty and derelict, it later sported signs proclaiming a site for a new garage, - but nothing happened to disturb its decay until demolition in 1981.

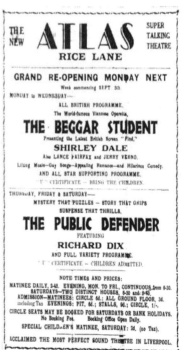

1955 Ad

ATLAS, Rice Lane.—Vincent Price in 'MAD MAGICIAN' (X), 6.30, 9.30. Also ' Bait ' (X).

THE NEW **ATLAS** RICE LANE SUPER TALKING THEATRE

GRAND RE-OPENING MONDAY NEXT

Week commencing SEPT. 5th

MONDAY to WEDNESDAY—

ALL BRITISH PROGRAMME.
The World-famous Viennese Operetta,

THE BEGGAR STUDENT

Presenting the Latest British Screen "Find,"

SHIRLEY DALE

Also LANCE FAIRFAX and JERRY VERNO.

Lilting Music—Gay Songs—Appealing Romance—and Hilarious Comedy.
AND ALL STAR SUPPORTING PROGRAMME.
'U' CERTIFICATE — BRING THE CHILDREN.

THURSDAY, FRIDAY & SATURDAY—

MYSTERY THAT PUZZLES — STORY THAT GRIPS
SUSPENSE THAT THRILLS.

THE PUBLIC DEFENDER

FEATURING

RICHARD DIX

AND FULL VARIETY PROGRAMME.
'U' CERTIFICATE — CHILDREN ADMITTED.

NOTE TIMES AND PRICES:

MATINEE DAILY, 2.45. EVENING, MON. TO FRI., CONTINUOUS from 6.30.
SATURDAYS—TWO DISTINCT HOUSES, 6.30 and 8.45.
ADMISSION—MATINEES: CIRCLE 5d.; ALL GROUND FLOOR, 3d.
including Tax EVENINGS: PIT, 5d.; STALLS, 9d.; CIRCLE, 1/-.
CIRCLE SEATS MAY BE BOOKED FOR SATURDAYS OR BANK HOLIDAYS.
No Booking Fee. Booking Office Open Daily.
SPECIAL CHILDREN'S MATINEE, SATURDAY: 2d. (no Tax).

ACCLAIMED THE MOST PERFECT SOUND THEATRE IN LIVERPOOL.

THE RITZ PICTURE HOUSE UTTING AVENUE ANFIELD

Independent, this 1120 seater stadium type opened in 1929. Showing later runs, due to circuit barring. Despite Cinemascope in 1955, it closed 2 years later, the first of the 'Supers' to go after only 28 years!

THE RITZ
PICTURE HOUSE, UTTING AVENUE, WALTON.

TREMENDOUS SUCCESS, WITH PACKED
HOUSE AT OPENING LAST SATURDAY.

TODAY (MONDAY), TUESDAY, WEDNESDAY,
THE JOKER.
Also
SAILORS DON'T CARE.
Preceded at 6.15 by
THE BETRAYAL.

MATINEE EVERY DAY AT 3, WITH FULL
ORCHESTRA.

RITZ, Utting Ave.—Sun cont 5-10 p.m.
Van Heflin, "THE RAID."
Also 'Bombers Moon' at 6.40.

After dereliction and being hacked about, it still exists as a sports shop. Above, in 1969. Right, in 1972, with the pillared entrance gone.

Final show on 30 June 1957 advert

THE RIVOLI AIGBURTH ROAD AIGBURTH

Built 1889 as the Sefton Park Assembly Rooms, it became a music hall showing animated pictures in the early 1900's. Remodelled in 1922.

Now with 600 seats , and renamed Rivoli, theatrical use continued until 1928, when Gaumont aquired it. Showing later runs, it was soon affected by diminishing attendances, closing in January 1957.

Kitchen showroom, 1980's

Last show before alterations, 19 August 1922

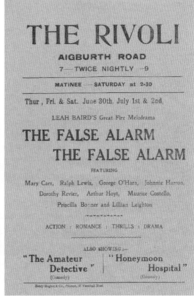

THE RIVOLI
AIGBURTH ROAD
7 — TWICE NIGHTLY — 9
MATINEE — SATURDAY at 2-30

Thur , Fri. & Sat. June 30th, July 1st & 2nd,

LEAH BAIRD'S Great Fire Melodrama

THE FALSE ALARM
THE FALSE ALARM

FEATURING

Mary Carr, Ralph Lewis, George O'Hara, Johnnie Harron, Dorothy Revier, Arthur Hoyt, Maurice Costello, Priscilla Bonner and Lillian Leighton

ACTION : ROMANCE : THRILLS : DRAMA

ALSO SHOWING :—

"The Amateur Detective"   "Honeymoon Hospital"

1927 poster

Unusually, it had a lady operator. Used for a church club, kitchen sales and is now a church.

Proscenium from box

THE ROSCOMMON PICTURE PALACE EVERTON

Originally built as a music hall in 1892, it became a cinema in 1911 with about 600 seats. Closed 13 December 1958, demolished 1980's

Like many former cinemas, it found a use as a garage and finally a firm of steel fabricators. When this 1980 picture was taken it was already awaiting demolition as was the rest of the area!
Colour views of the lesser halls are a rarity, so this is worth a look.

THE ROYAL HIPPODROME WEST DERBY ROAD

This enormous building was originally a theatre, seating 3,500. It opened in 1902 but was converted to a cinema in 1931.

Gaumont aquired it in 1928. The proscenium width was 40 feet. Unviable, due to its size, closure was in May 1970, then derelict until demolition in 1981. The site was originally Henglers Circus building. Gallery patrons had to queue in the side street, left side.

Below, With Cinemascope

Above, The auditorium layout.
Right, Gallery entrance in 1931

THE ROYAL HIPPODROME continued

Four sad pictures of its demolition. Although in its death throes, the ornate decorations still convey an air of dignity in 1980. Judging by the mess, it looks like hippos were being used to demolish it! The 'Higgys' pub next door has now met a similar fate!

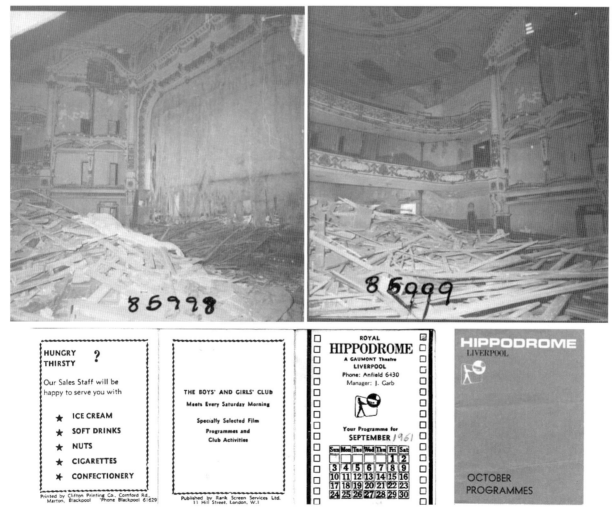

THE ROYAL BRECK ROAD EVERTON

A former music hall, becoming a cinema in 1920. Essoldo from 1954, it lasted until 1965, then bingo. Currently a furniture shop.

This 1985 shot shows the cropped facade. All the widows are bricked up as an anti-scally measure for the insurance. The auditorium is offset to the entrance, being wider behind the pub on the right.

Currently a false ceiling is installed at balcony level, with just the curve showing, above being derelict

The very narrow proscenium dominates this 1981 view from the balcony. Cinemascope was installed in 1955, though unsuitable!
Note the boxes on only one side.

This is a really a typical suburban music hall, being long and narrow. Note the stalls floor rake (below)

THE SAVOY WEST DERBY ROAD

Picture Allen Eyles Collection

Between the Olympia and the Hippodrome, this 890 seater opened in 1914. Under Gaumont from 1928, showing later runs. Cinemascope was installed, but was not effective and it closed in September 1958.

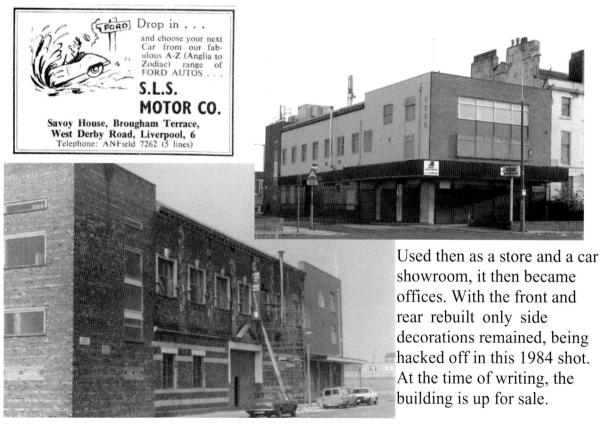

Used then as a store and a car showroom, it then became offices. With the front and rear rebuilt only side decorations remained, being hacked off in this 1984 shot. At the time of writing, the building is up for sale.

THE SCALA LIME STREET

Only having 650 seats, including a balcony, it opened in January 1916. Decorated in the 'Egyptian' style, it was independant,, though leased to Fox to show their Cinemascope films from 1954 - 60.

Then leased to Gala Films for 'X' rated movies, ABC bought it in 1968. Closed in 1982, due to the Forum tripling, it was then the Hippodrome club, now X in the City.

Original facade was rebuilt following bomb damage.

As new. The balcony wings were later removed for Cinemascope

SHORT LIVED VENUES
WESTMINSTER HALL CINEMA SMITH STREET KIRKDALE

Formerly a music hall, leased in 1908 by the Weisker brothers for a cinema conversion. It seated about 650, with a side balcony.
Re-named the Doric in 1932, it was destroyed in a 1941 air raid.

THE GARSTON PICTUREDROME HEALD STREET

Built as an roller skating rink, the building on the left showed pictures between 1910 and 1923. As the Winter Gardens dance hall until 1966, site now houses.

Right, 1900's view.
1960 advert below

ELECTRIC PICTURE PALACE BRIDGE Rd LITHERLAND

Built as the Assembly Rooms at the beginning of the 20th century, furniture auctions by the founder of what was to become Outhwaite and Litherland were also held here. It was converted to a cinema in 1910. When it opened it was the only cinema in Seaforth and Litherland. Sadly, the building was destroyed by fire on Sunday 13 July 1913.

SHORT LIVED VENUES continued.

THE BURLINGTON VAUXHALL ROAD/BURLINGTON STREET

Opening in 1926, this stadium type seated 1100, with its length along Vauxhall Road. The lease expired in 1937, a wartime store in 1941 and demolished, then part of Tate & Lyles

THE PREMIER PICTURE PALACE 233 SMITHDOWN ROAD

Scally cut off stamp!

Built as a billiard hall in the 1890's, the downstairs became a cinema 1912. Closing in 1923 or 4, the building reverted to its former use and was demolished by 1952, a house taking its place.

THE ADELPHI THEATRE CHRISTIAN STREET

An 1846 built small theatre, which became a cinema from 1912 to 1921. Replaced by the nearby New Adelphi, which see.

Demolition in progress in 1921. The fire brigade were called to this blaze
Note the pillar balcony supports.

THE SMITHDOWN PICTURE PLAYHOUSE SMITHDOWN ROAD

Opened in February 1915, by a company of the same name, it seated about 1000 including a balcony. Lasting until 11 September 1963.

June 1953, the Coronation flags are out.

Above, projection room with new Kalee projectors.

SMITHDOWN PICTURE PLAYHOUSE
S 'APACHE' (U) Tech. Jean Peters &
Burt Lancaster, Mats. 2.30. Cont. 6.

There is very little about this one, certainly no facade pictures. Advertising in the 'Echo' like this May 1955 one above and the bingo bit opposite is all that is left.

Re-opened as a bingo club 6 days later, this was short lived and by 1968 the building had been replaced by a supermarket, featured in the Toxteth Riots

'MARTHA' AND 'MINNIE' TO OPEN BINGO HALL

FALLING attendances at films and big demands for Bingo games have forced a Wavertree cinema to close down after 48 years—and open up again as a Bingo Hall.

The last film star to appear at the Smithdown Picture Playhouse is Joanne Woodward in "Woman of Summer"—now showing—but next Tuesday two more stars will be there to open the Smithdown Bingo Club.

They are Martha Longhurst and Minnie Caldwell of "Coronation Street," who will take part in the first Bingo game.

A Wavertree man who attended the first film at the cinema 50 years ago, Mr. Ernest Mercer, will be the guest of honour at the opening.

A spokesman for the firm said this week: "The demand for membership of the club has been overwhelming, and that is the reason for the switch. If we had had the same demand for films, the building would have continued as a cinema."

SOME OTHER EARLY PLACES THAT SHOWED FILMS
This is not a full list, but examples of short lived venues still existing.

CROSBY CINEMA LIVERPOOL ROAD CROSBY

This was St Lukes church hall, converted into a 500 seat cinema in 1913. Periods of closure followed, the last advertising for it in July 1916, a hall again by 1919. Later next door to the Regent, the wall on the left.

LATHOM HALL PICTURE PALACE
Situated on Lathom Avenue, Seaforth, this was built as a public hall in 1884. Converted to a cinema, it opened in June 1912 and was another 300 seater. Despite initial success, with large crowds, it was eclipsed by other larger cinemas opening nearby. The war did not help, either, and it closed about 1916. The building had several subsequent uses, until the present one

THE STANLEY HALL
On Prescot Road, near the abbatoir, this former billiards hall opened as a cinema in 1910. Closure was abruptly in 1915, then reverting to billiards which lasted until the Second World War.
Currently a dance studio and shops..

These buildings are still extant in 2010, all quite small halls.

THE STELLA PICTURE HOUSE SEAFORTH ROAD SEAFORTH

Seating 1200, this opened in December 1920. Independent, then part of the Bedford Cinemas circuit, later run films being shown. As more modern cinemas opened nearby, audiences dwindled, closing in 1958.

Demolished May 1964 for the Stella Shopping Precinct. This old postcard gives a clue to its location. The Palladium was further along.

THE ST. JAMES PICTUREDROME ST. JAMES STREET

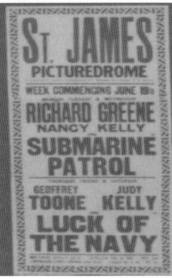

Opening in March 1914, this 870 seater stadium type originally had an ornate facade, including a column supported dome. A modern frontage replaced this in the 1950's,(top right picture) but it closed in March 1960, being demolished for road improvements.

SEFTON PARK PICTUREDROME

On Smithdown Road, formerly stables for tramway horses, it was converted in 1911 into a 300 seat cinema. Gaumont controlled from 1928, it closed the following year, as they also owned the nearby Grand

Only this panelling above a fire door and the cast iron heating pipes remain from its former use. The two square windows had the projection room behind.

THE SWAN PICTUREDROME MILL LANE OLD SWAN

An early purpose built stadium, seating 1000, it opened in April 1916.

1987 and in 1995

With a 35 foot wide proscenium and an 8 foot deep stage, variety acts were featured during the 1920's. As an independent, restricted to late runs and off circuit, it closed July 1956, later bingo and clubs.

After demolition, the mosaic foyer floor and rubbish tip!

THE TATLER NEWS THEATRE, CHURCH STREET

Seating 600, it was opened in 1934. The auditorium was at the rear of the shops, with just a narrow entrance and canopy on Church Street. Best remembered as a cartoon cinema, it became part of Classic in 1968 and despite trying different types of films, only as a club cinema with uncensored films seemed to be successful. Closure was on 31 March 1973. Solitaire, a clothes shop, used it next, but odd fragments of its past still linger, like the plaster below.

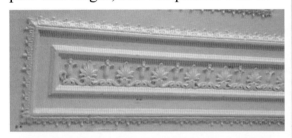

The top view is from 1955, the lower after closure in 1973

THEATRES SHOWING FILMS
This was to boost income when live theatre was struggling.

The ornate interior of the Pavilion on Lodge Lane, from 1980.
Sadly, it was destroyed by fire in 1986.
Left, below, the Shakespeare in Fraser Street also went up in flames in 1976.

The Royal Court in 1980

The David Lewis, St James's Place in 1977, demolished for new road.

THE TROCADERO CAMDEN STREET

Provincial Cinematograph Theatres opened this 1347 seater in 1922.
Re-named Gaumont in 1950, though under their control since 1930. Showing first runs, while the London Road Odeon did roadshows, the twinning and then quadrupling of the latter made it superflous to Rank, who closed it in May 1974. Demolished 1996, after snooker club use.

Above View from Christian Street in 1966.
Other pictures when new.

THE TUNNEL ROAD PICTUREDROME EDGE HILL

Near the junction with Edge Lane, the licence was granted in December 1914. With 840 seats, it was an independent for all it's life.

Showing mainly thrillers and westerns, it was renamed the Avenue in July 1961, closing in December 1968 due to a road widening scheme.

In 1980, as a bingo club, the road scheme was cancelled. Became the Tunnel Club in the 1980's, finally demolished after a fire in 1995.

A 1924 flyer   1948, with the cinema on the right

I have included the Tunnel Road picture to show how much has changed!

THE VICTORIA CHERRY AVENUE WALTON

A 1923 stadium type cinema ending up in the Essoldo fold after 1954. Named Essoldo in 1957, it closed in August 1963, becoming a bingo club. Currently a window manufacturer These 1986 views show the external in 'Top Flight' colours and the interior detailing.

This shows the former projection room, which now contains a gas fired warm air heater. The grilles are at the sides and the fake windows.
A false ceiling was later installed, forever hiding the ceiling and upper proscenium.

THE VICTORY PICTURE HOUSE WALTON ROAD

Opened in 1922, this seated 1130 and was on the corner of Luton Grove. ABC aquired it in 1935, along with the nearby Astoria.

Towner images

Awful frontage picture!

February 1931 advert and internal badge

It opened with just this advert in the "Echo" on 4 October 1922.

Screening later runs, re-issues and less popular releases, despite Cinemascope in 1955, closure came on 29 July 1961. Demolished that winter, replaced by a row of shops. Unusually, the auditorium was not symmetrical, being wider to the right and so was the balcony, as seen in these 1951 views.

IT'S THE END OF THE ROAD FOR THE VICTORY CINEMA

The curtains will fall and the lights dim for the final time to-morrow night (Saturday) when the Victory Cinema, Walton Road, will bow her way out from the world of entertainment.

WALTON VALE PICTURE HOUSE WALTON VALE

Erected by a company of the same name in 1922, capacity was 1150. With only the Palace for competition, it survived until January 1959, Cinemascope being installed in 1955. The Palace only lasted until 27 June of the same year!

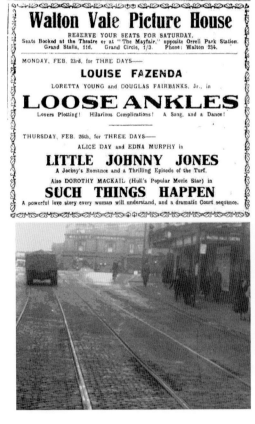

1933, 1947 aerial and 1952 views

THE WARWICK WINDSOR STREET TOXTETH

A very basic small (437 seater) hall, dating from 1911, at the junction of Stananought Street. An independent, it closed in 1958.

In 1963, it was a club, but the original facade is intact.

By June 1967 it had become the Starlight Club. Note the reduction in height, resulting in the oddly cropped frontage!

This newspaper cutting also from 1963, shows it as the Talk of the Town club. A talking point it certainly was, with the owner denying the complaints. The frontage is already different than the top left picture.

Residents complain of rows and fights by late night revellers

Finally demolished in 1982

THE WARWICK continued

In 1955 an accident occurred when part of the balcony ceiling collapsed during a performance, injuring several people. Spare seats had been stored in the ceiling void, but the weight proved too much!

The basic auditorium, with not even a ceiling! The condition was typical of the poorer halls. You can understand the draw of TV!

Just look at how many seats will Fit into the void!

The extent of the collapse. This ceiling 'squared off' the underside of the projection box

THE WEST DERBY PICTURE HOUSE, ALMONDS GREEN

A 950 seater stadium type, opening on 30 July 1927. Aquired by Cheshire County Cinemas in 1946, re-named Plaza November 1955.

Sketch of the original facade and a partial view from January 1952

As in 2008

1967 as Tesco's

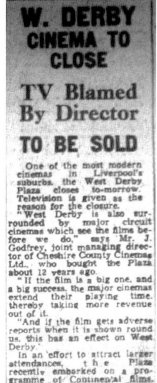

W. DERBY CINEMA TO CLOSE
TV Blamed By Director
TO BE SOLD

One of the most modern cinemas in Liverpool's suburbs, the West Derby Plaza closes to-morrow. Television is given as the reason for the closure.

"West Derby is also surrounded by major circuit cinemas which see the films before we do," says Mr. J. Godfrey, joint managing director of Cheshire County Cinemas Ltd., who bought the Plaza about 12 years ago.

"If the film is a big one, and a big success, the major cinemas extend their playing time, thereby taking more revenue out of it.

"And if the film gets adverse reports when it is shown round us, this has an effect on West Derby.'

In an effort to attract larger attendances, the Plaza recently embarked on a programme of Continental films, but this was not successful.

Closed in January 1960, in 1963 it was a showroom/warehouse, then a supermarket who rebuilt the front.

THE WINTER GARDENS CHURCH STREET WATERLOO

Formerly a gym then a billiard hall, it became a cinema in 1909 but was a theatre following major alterations in 1922. Again a cinema with 655 seats from 1931, it lasted independently until 1965.

The original first cinema facade and the final form as prior to closure in 1965.

WINTER GARDENS, WATERLOO, continued

Posters announcing final programme, closing after Matinee, Saturday 4 Sept. 1965, no evening dance!
Built out projection room and interior in 1945.
Final facade for short lived bingo.
Sold 1982 for Kingsway Church Centre.

THE WOOLTON PICTURE HOUSE MASON STREET WOOLTON
A stadium type, with 900 seats and opening in September 1927.

The canopy is altered for a film, February 2009

1963 programme

Cheshire County Cinemas aquired it in 1954, installing Cinemascope the following year, with the widescreen in front of the proscenium. In 1984, re-seating reduced the capacity to 256.

Following the death of the last owner, David Wood, it closed in September 2006.

WOOLTON.—Edmund O'Brien in 'THE SHANGHAI STORY' (A). Also 'Laughing Anne' (7.26 only). Cont. 5.45.

Reopening in March 2007 under new owners, it survives as a family cinema.

WHAT NEXT?

With cinema admissions rising again, despite the lure of the Home Cinema, the multiplex would appear to be the way forward.

Having more in common with industrial units, plus huge car parks, the interiors have nothing in common with a traditional cinema, being a neon temple to the god of food! The auditoriums are comfortable but basic. Even the screen curtains don't move Like it or hate it, this is films survival kit!

Trocadero

Kings

Paramount/Odeon

THAT'S ALL FOLKS

This was the fate of the majority of the cinemas, now you would never know that they ever existed. I hope that this book has reminded you of what has been. When it's gone - it's gone FOREVER

Palais de Luxe

Astoria

Bedford

Odeon London Road

Prince of Wales